America's Guns and
the Second Amendment

A Momentous Decision by the United States Supreme Court

Jamie Lucier, Ph.D.

authorHOUSE®

AuthorHouse™
1663 Liberty Drive
Bloomington, IN 47403
www.authorhouse.com
Phone: 1-800-839-8640

First published by AuthorHouse 7/14/2009

ISBN: 978-1-4389-7104-9 (sc)

Printed in the United States of America
Bloomington, Indiana

This book is printed on acid-free paper.

This book is dedicated to the memory of
Vianette Mungarro

[1979-1993]

-Remembrance

A bright, innocent fourteen-year-old girl was just doing what fourteen year-old girls do. She was visiting with her friends in the front yard at her home, probably talking mostly about young boys. Suddenly, two boys from another neighborhood approached and threatened the girls because of their association with others from a rival gang. Shots were first fired into the air. Then, as she tried hard to run away, the fourteen-year-old girl was shot in the back. With blood gushing from her chest, the child tried to get into the front door of her home. Calling for help, she cried. "They killed me, mama! They killed me!"

Lying on her back, her head cradled in her mother's arms, the young girl's eyes glazed over as the life left her body. "Mi hija, mi hija (My daughter, my daughter!") the mother wailed, as the two young men ran off. Unconsolable, wailing and sobbing for most of the night, the girl's grieving mother paced around the yard, unable to leave the area where her beloved daughter had been murdered. A neighbor agonized over how to handle her own feelings. "What was terrible was that the child's mother just couldn't be consoled," she said. "All of us in the neighborhood lay in bed, hearing her crying all night long for her little girl who was dead"

This book is sincerely dedicated to the memory of that innocent child and to her mother.

The child's name was Vianette.

The Author

Table of Contents

INTRODUCTION

Many of us recall the good old days when we spent a cool Saturday morning tromping over the hills or through the woods carrying a hex-barreled .22 rifle or dad's vintage sixteen-gauge shotgun. What fun it was, plinking at tin cans, poppin' at squirrels or prairie dogs or knocking doves out of the sky. Or maybe we remember the bitter cold we endured as we hunted for deer, all the while wondering why we hadn't stayed home where it was warm. Then came the heart pounding excitement we felt as we sighted in on that beautiful three-point buck, the one we dropped with a perfect shot from our lever action 30 - 30.

Those were the good old days - the days when hunting was fun and safe, when guns were used for sport and hunting instead of self protection. Today it's different It seems now as though people are about as likely to use guns to shoot one another as they are to hunt for game. That isn't really true, of course. Hundreds of thousands of guns are used every day in perfectly legitimate sporting activities, hunting and target practice, gun club—sanctioned marksmanship competitions and for the protection of personal property and families by law enforcement personnel and law- abiding citizens.

It is true, however, that there are an awful lot of gun killings going on all across America, many more than the average citizen knows about and certainly far more than would be occurring if only existing gun laws were more effectively enforced and if the public were better advised of the responsibilities associated with gun ownership.

Many people die because guns fall into the hands of the wrong kinds of people. They are used in robberies, home invasions, gang warfare as well as planned murders. While they are in the hands of some law-abiding citizens, guns often accidently kill family members or friends, sometimes very young children. Many lives are lost because guns are readily available at times when tempers flare or when alcohol or drugs reduce the frustrated person's ability to maintain controL Yet, many would argue that guns serve to protect the law-abiding citizen from the criminal and that the times when an armed person prevents violence offset many times over those occasions when a gun is used to kill an innocent person. Indeed, some well-versed executives from the gun lobby have stressed for years their belief that the best deterrent against crime in America is a well-armed citizenry.

In the 1940s and 1950s, there were roughly 75 million guns in the hands of private American citizens. At the turn of the century that number had increased to approximately 220 million and the number is still growing. Guns are everywhere. Every day they are being carried by the thousands into drug stores, banks, malls, parks, stadiums and movie theaters. They are in homes, businesses, under the seats of automobiles, in mens' pockets and ladies' purses and in the backpacks of some school children. They are in home safes, closets not so safe, in night stands, dresser drawers and under mattresses. Some protect the innocent. Unfortunately, many kill the innocent.

Most gun owners store and use their guns in a wise manner. They are safety conscious citizens, independent thinkers who cherish their freedoms. They will stand firmly in defense of their perceived right to bear arms. Some are collectors of vintage weapons who are very fascinated by the high quality precision workmanship that goes into the design and manufacturing of guns. They collect them as a dealer would collect fine artwork or an automobile enthusiast would invest in a variety of very valuable classic cars. To the avid collector, those cherished possessions reflect and convey an enduring sense of history.

Most gun owners are just plain everyday people who like to hunt, who enjoy shooting as a sport or just want to ensure the protection of their families. They wouldn't think of harming anyone and they tend to resent being seen as a threat that must be curbed by a lessening of their personal freedoms.

For pleasure or for sport, for a study of history or for protection alone, the gun is seen today as a significant part of the American zeitgeist. There is no denying that America is armed. Whether that fact is seen as good or bad, advisable or ill-advised, it should be accepted that the average American family is, indeed, in arms way.

American Gun Death Statistics

On average, 82 Americang die each day from gunfire.

+ Each year between 1993 and 1997, an average of 1,621 murderers under age eighteen took someone's life with a gun.

+ In 2003, only 163 justifiable homicides occurred by private citizens using handguns in the United States. Overall that year, more than 28,000 people died from gunfire. That's 2,300 per month, 575 per week.

+ The presence of a handgun in the home triples the risk of homicide in the home.

+ The presence of a handgun in the home increases the risk of suicide five-fold.

+ In the year 2001, murders by firearm included:

New Zealand 6

Japan 56

Great Britian 96

Canada 168

Germany 338

United States 11,348

Sources: WISQARS, National Center for Injury Protection and Control, Injury Mortality Reports, N England .1 Mcd, 1992, 1993.

Jamie Lucier, Ph.D.

A comparison of American war deaths with Civilian firearms deaths *within* America

1981 - 2007

War deaths

ElSalvador	(1980—1992)	20
Beirut	(1982 — 1984)	266
Persian Gulf	(1987 - 1988)	39
Granada	(1983)	19
Panama	(1989)	40
Gulf War	(1991)	269
Somalia	(1992 — 1993)	43
Bosnia	(1995)	12
Afghanistan	(2002 - 2008)	482
Iraq	(2003- 2008)	4230
Total		<u>5,420</u>

Civilian deaths

1981	34,050	1991	38,317		
1982	32,957	1992	37,776	2001	29,573
1983	31,099	1993	39,595	2002	30,242
1984	31,331	1994	38,505	2003	30,136
1985	31,566	1995	35,957	2004	29,569
1986	33,373	1996	34,040	2005	29,000*
1987	32,895	1997	32,436	2006	29,000*
1988	33,989	1998	30,708	2007	29.000*
1989	34,776	1999	28,874		
1990	37,155	2000	28,663		
* Estimated Total			<u>884,582</u>		

Note: For every war-related death since 1980, more than 160 Americans died from gunfire *within* their own country.

Source: Department of Justice Bureau of Justice Statistics

Chapter One

Guns: A Problem
or a Part of the Solution?

It's difficult to imagine that anyone would buy a gun assuming that its possession would likely result in sadness or harm to friends or loved-ones. Instead, the usual gun owner purchases his or her weapon confident that it will have entertainment value and also that it will provide the added benefit of increased security in the event of personal threat to his or her family.

While surveying the ads in the gun magazines and touring the gun shops, the prospective purchaser seeks information about the gun that will have the best design, that handles best, is most accurate and has a reputation for being the most dependable. He searches for the weapon that would most effectively meet his personal needs.

The magazines are filled with enthusiasm and excitement about the thrill of the hunt, the out-of-doors, the wild animals that serve as game for the skilled marksman who prides himself with his trophies. The hunter may be shown next to the head of the elk or wild boar that the taxidermist has prepared for mounting above the fireplace in the family den.

The hunter prides himself on his marksmanship skills, often spending his weekends sighting in his favorite rifle. He tunes in his scope to get round after round into the center of target after target, all in preparation for that special day, the beginning of deer or elk season and that special sight of his prey, drawn close by the lens that shrinks the yardage.

Many times the possession and display of a gun serve to dissuade anyone who might otherwise take unlawful advantage of an unarmed citizen. Many stories are told of the armed law-abiding citizen who successfully defends his property or his family with his handgun. Gun advocates are quick to seize on these examples and use them as evidence of the wisdom of gun ownership.

Indeed, it has been suggested by some criminologists that firearms are used successfully for protection as many as 2.5 million times per year! If this is true, it is a very persuasive claim. The fear that the law-abiding citizen might be armed is seen as a very significant deterrent against potential assault or injury by the criminal. This is often true of course, and it is not difficult to find cases where gun owners have protected their property and their families with the convincing aid of a handgun or shotgun.

But, 2.5 million times per year? Writers against various forms of gun regulation are often too quick to accept claims such as these as though they are established facts. Consider how easy it is to just accept this conjecture as fact, without challenging the manner in which the data have been collected and the real validity of the conclusions that have been drawn. Proceeding logically from the assumption that the truth has been established, some pro-gun activists build an elaborate case for the arming of greater and greater numbers of citizens who then provide the public with greater protection from the ravages of the criminal element. One might wonder if it is really true, however, that as more and more citizens are armed, more criminals are dissuaded from committing crimes.

How does one establish as a fact that 2.5 million times per year a gun is successfully used for protection? Does one count the times? Does the researcher use telephone surveys? Representative samples? Police records?

How is it possible to verify the accuracy of these types of data? It is not possible; Any use of these statistics as facts should be viewed as highly suspect. This does not mean that it doesn't occur. It does happen quite frequently, but perhaps its frequency of occurrence is much overstated and certainly its frequency of occurrence should be considered against the often understated (or stated not at all) cost of gun ownership in lost lives of innocent people.

If there is an inverse correlation between the number of guns owned by law-abiding citizens and the crime rate (e g, the more citzens have guns, the less the crime), then America by sheer volume of gun ownership, should have the lowest crime rate in the world. It would seem that the neighborhoods of America should be the safest anywhere. Are they?

People kill themselves or others with guns in America at the rate of approximately 30,000 per year The statistics vary from year to year with the worst toll being the 39,595 who died from gunfire in the peak year of 1993 These are statistics that are rarely ever shown in books written by those who object to most gun-regulation. On a yearly basis the Federal Bureau of Investigation compiles its statistics on violence and on crime with its annual survey of cases reported by over 17,000 law enforcement agencies nationwide.

United States Firearm Deaths *

1990	37,155	* Source:
1995	35,957	National Center for Injury Protection and Control
2002	30,242	

While the toll of 30,242 deaths from gunfire in the year 2002 would seem to reflect a positive trend, it remains clear that the price of gun ownership by both the law-abiding and the unlawful remains tragically high. Just consider the fact that in 2001 the death toll from the terrible terrorist attack on the Twin Towers of the New York World Trade Center was 2,976. That means that during the following year over ten times as many people were killed by gunfire in America as compared to the number who died on Sept. 11, 2001!

Consider the gun-death toll of 30,242 in another way. It is equivalent to the number of lives that would be lost if an airliner carrying over 240 passengers were to crash into the streets, mountains and fields of America every third day for the entire year!

Members of the gun lobby would advise that these tragic numbers would be significantly increased were it not for the fact that the law-abiding citizens are free to arm themselves against the threat posed by the criminal element. They may be right in their assessment But in order to prove this point conclusively it would be necessary to provide evidence more convincing than the conjecture of pro-gun activists. The truth is that there is no strong and conclusive evidence that can settle the issue either way at this time.

The research and extrapolation presented by those interested in supporting the pro-gun stance on this matter may be somewhat tainted by motivated bias. However, it would be unwise to simply dismiss completely the role that the gun can play in securing personal safrty. A wise researcher proceeds with caution, neither affirming nor rejecting a hypothesis until the data reveal conclusions that are supportable beyond the realms of bias and chance influence. The case has not been made, for or against the gun safety idea.

Gunfire is not the most significant contributor to death in America related to conditions other than disease. Clearly, automobile accidents are listed as most costly, as indicated by the chart below:

American Deaths in 2000 * (unrelated to disease)

Traffic Accidents	41,994	
Alcohol-related		* Source:
Traffic Accidents	17,448	National Center for Injury Protection and Control
Firearms	28,663	
Drownings	4,073	

Are America's guns a problem or are they a part of the solution? It would appear that the answer depends on whom you ask. Ask a gun industry lobbyist and you get reassuring confirmation of the contribution that guns make to the security of your property and your family. If you ask the family members who attended the funerals of those who died from gunfire, you will be apt to get a different point of view.

Chapter Two

It Depends On Whom You Ask

George Fados was driving home from work one afternoon in a rather remote area on the fringe of the City of Los Angeles when he observed a man struggling with a young woman, trying to force her into his car. The woman was screaming, trying desperately to escape, but the man wouldn't let her go. Without hesitation, George grabbed the handgun that he usually carried under the seat of his truck and went to the poor woman's aid.

Seeing an armed man approaching, the assailant released the woman, got into his car and sped away. A rape and even a possible homicide were avoided because, fortunately, an armed law-abiding citizen saw what was happening and was quick to respond with the threat of force.

In November of 1993, Carl James and Taz Pell accosted Arthur Boone, of Brooklyn, N. Y., demanding money in an armed robbery. Boone, however, was armed with a handgun. He killed both of his assailants. One month earlier, the home of 92 year-old Bessie Jones, of Chicago, illinois, was burglarized by a teen-ager. Although in a wheelchair, Bessie took advantage of a moment of distraction by the taunting, threatening sixteen year-old and shot him dead with a .38 revolver.

As reported on the Donahue television show in November, 2002 (MSNBC) Susan Gonzalez didn't want guns in her home. Her husband, however, insisted on keeping a handgun. Two masked men broke into their home at 4:40 AM and shot both Susan and her husband. Susan managed to get her husband's gun and killed one of the intruders, scaring off the other. A month later, the other one was apprehended. Now, Susan holds a carry-concealed permit in the State of Florida.

These are all cases of personal gun ownership that resulted in a consequence that most would see as a defense of the freedoms of law-abiding citizens under threat. Many cases could be cited as evidence of the wisdom in being an armed person. Clearly, some people would have died had there not been an armed citizen there to see that justice was served.

There is, surely, another side to this story. It is the tragic story of the significant number of innocent people who are killed by someone who legally owns a weapon and inadvertently, out of frustration, in a fit of rage or by accident, manages to destroy the freedom of an innocent person.

In Phoenix, Arizona, a young couple entered 1-17, one of the busy freeways, unintentionally cutting in front of a sports car traveling the same route. They soon noticed that the two men in the car were pulling up beside them on the right.The man sitting opposite the driver raised a rifle and fired into the side of the couple's pickup.

The young woman slumped over onto her husband's lap, a bullet having struck her in the side of her head.The husband quickly turned off of the freeway. In indescribable panic, he drove to the nearest business, a convenience store, where he cried out for help that came too late. Jennifer died. So did the couple's unborn child.

Two young teen-agers burst into a Picadilly Cafeteria and forced a frightened twenty-year-old manager to unlock the safe. One of the gunmen had an Uzi-type pistol. The other had a semi-automatic handgun. Irritated because he took too much time to open the safe, one of the gunmen fired a shot into the back of the young man's head. Stephan Simpson died as he struggled to meet the demands of the two armed thugs.

Padriac "Patrick" Hill, age 20, was working his usual late shift at a United Artists Discount Cinema. Hill and three of his fellow employees were ordered to get on the floor as three armed men demanded money. Patrick tried to explain that no one had the combination to the safe. He, too, was shot in the head. Another employee, shot through the shoulder, survived by playing dead.

A six-year-old child accompanied her aunt on a ride to the carwash to clean the family sedan. Before washing the car, the aunt proceeded to vacuum the interior while the child watched. At one point the hose of the vacuum knocked a loaded revolver off of the front seat. When the gun hit the pavement, it fired, killing the child instantly. During the panic that followed, the aunt had to be forcibly restrained by others as she tried to get to the gun so that she could shoot herself, so grieved was she by what she had done to her brother's child.

A fourteen year-old girl and her boyfriend were wandering in the Arizona desert when they came upon a lady camping alone at one of the campsites. The lady, who was in her fifties, was befriended by the young couple. However, the young man wanted proof of the girl's love for him, so he coerced the girl into killing their new friend. She complied by pumping bullets into the back of the innocent woman.

This same young man was convicted as one of two men who executed six Buddhist monks, a nun, a novice and a temple helper in their temple near Phoenix, Arizona several months earlier, making them lie still while each was shot in the back of the head.

Two young rowdies were ejected from a nightclub by an oversized security guard because they had been noisy and annoying to the other patrons. They had consumed too much alcohol. Six people died as the men sprayed the area with bullets when they returned to vent their revenge.

A five-year-old boy found the gun that mommy kept on her nightstand in her bedroom. His two year-old sister is no longer with them.

On October 28, 2002, nursing student Robert Stewart Flores quietly entered a classroom at the University of Arizona School of Nursing and started shooting. Nursing Professors Barbara Monroe, Cheryl McGaffic and Robin Rogers all died at the scene. Flores then killed himself. The highly troubled student, who was tending toward failure in the program, had on occasion boasted about his concealed-carry permit to carry a handgun.

A mother of four made her husband so angry during a loud family argument that he lost control and shot two of their children, then his wife. In despair, he then killed himself with a shot to the head. One child survived. The other child and her mother died at the scene.

Rudolph Garcia, a loving, considerate grandfather suffered the loss of his daughter Sharon, just age 19, in a drive-by shooting at a local city park.

Then, only a few months later, Garcia's grandson, Michael Mendivil, was killed in a gang-related shooting as he left a pizza parlor. As a reaction to these tragedies, two deaths in his family in a matter of only several months, the elder Garcia became an anti-gang activist in his own neighborhood.

A year later, while attending his son's wedding, Rudolph himself died accidently from a gunshot wound. Someone fired a weapon, thinking that he was being fired on by the occupants of a red pickup that was driving by. The one who fired the .380 handgun was Rudolph's own son! He had purchased the weapon for protection of his own family. Then, he accidently killed his own father! Police found no evidence of any weapons in the red pickup.

A young visiting foreign student from Japan, who was unable to speak English, appeared one evening at the home of a typical family in a quiet residential neighborhood in the State of Louisiana. He and a friend were dressed in Halloween costumes. Inadvertently, he had rung the doorbell at a home several houses down from the one where the party was located.

The lady who answered the door panicked. She screamed for her husband to "Get the gun!" The armed law-abiding citizen demanded that the boy "Freeze!" Yoshi Hattori didn't understand the command and was killed as he moved forward to ask directions to the party. The law-abiding citizen was tried for manslaughter. A year later, Masaich and Mieko Hattori, the sad parents of sixteen-year-old Yoshi presented President Bill Clinton with a quarter of a million signatures from Japanese citizens who appealed to him to end the gun violence in America. 230 died from gunfire in Japan in 1993, 40,230 died in America!

An innocent fourteen year-old girl was doing what teen-age girls usually do, visiting with her friends in the front yard at her home. Suddenly, two young boys approached and threatened the girls because of their association with others from a rival gang. Shots were first fired into the air. Then, as she tried to run away, Vianette Mungarro was shot in the back. With blood gushing from her chest, the child tried to get into the front door of her home. Calling for help, she cried, "They killed me, mama! They killed me!"

Lying on her back, her head cradled in her mother's arms, Vianette's eyes glazed over as the life left her body. "Mi hija, mi hija" ("My daughter, my daughter!") the mother wailed as the two young men ran off. Unconsolable, wailing and sobbing for most of the night, the child's mother paced around the yard, unable to leave the area where her beloved daughter had been murdered. A neighbor agonized over how to handle her own feelings, "What was terrible was that Vianette's poor mother just couldn't be consoled," she said. "All of us in the neighborhood lay in bed, hearing her crying all night for her little girl who was dead"

It is said that thousands of lives have been saved because an armed citizen was on the scene, being at the right place at the right time. There's no denying it. When robbers are shooting at innocent bystanders in a bank, it would be great if an armed citizen could take them out in short order. Who, when living, under the threat of being killed, wouldn't prefer to be armed in order to protect himself?

Yet, the fact that millions and millions of people are living in arms way may be a part of what is actually escalating the threat. Would you "need" to carry a gun in your car if you knew that very few cars had guns in them?

Do more guns in homes and cars make it safer to be in your home or in your car? Are there more times that a gun is used resulting in the saving of life than the taking of innocent life?

The answers to these difficult questions depend entirely on whom you ask. Request an answer from any of the active representatives of the gun lobby and you will be assured that guns provide a positive protective influence in modern society. They will claim that trained persons who legally carry concealed weapons tend to constrain the criminals who fear the deadly potential consequence of facing an armed law-abiding citizen.

Others will claim that the potential harm that can come to any family in which guns are kept is as much as six times greater than is the case in families where no guns are present. On the Donahue Show, Michael Barnes, President of the Brady Campaign to Prevent Gun Violence, claimed that a handgun is as much as 22 times more likely to be used against a family member or a friend than against a burglar or intruder. "Buy a gun," he says, "and you increase the risk to your family. You do not reduce it," he says. "Gun ownership will not make you safer."

Who is correct? Well, it depends on whom you ask. One thing is for sure, those who want more gun regulation are not inclined to point out the number of instances in which a gun has been used successfully to prevent tragedy. And no gun lobbyist is going to write willingly about the total number of people who die each year from gunfire in America.

Chapter Three

Damned Liars and Statisticians

No subject has the power to get more people more riled, irritated and downright angry than the issue of gun control. Just watch an afternoon television talk show with an invited guest expounding on the problems of gun violence and crime. You will see a rather disturbed audience. The guest on any given day could be a representative of the National Rifle Association. He would come to the session armed to the teeth with statistical arguments against any significant increase in gun regulation.

"Gun laws rarely work," he would say, as he pointed to the useless laws in Washington, D. C. where tight restrictions have little effect on crime rates. "Across the nation, we have over 20,000 gun laws! Why not enforce the ones we have, instead of forcing the law-abiding citzens to give up more of their freedoms." You would be dazzled by how well-informed the guest is and find yourself overwhelmed by his rapid-fire presentation of statistical facts that support the unlimited, constitutionally guaranteed right to keep and bear arms.

If the guest that day appeared as a representative of the Brady Campaign Against Gun Violence, an equal number of statistical arguments would be used to convince you that the United States is permeated with guns, that they are being used to destroy children, devastate families and that most of the nation's citizens are living in fear. Attention would be focused on other areas of the nation where gun laws have been successful in reducing the rate of crime and violence.

Lobbyists on each side of any issue learn to select from the available data only those statistics that promote their own points of view and to avoid the use of any that might tend to confuse the issue and make their own version of the truth less clear. Gun proponents might enjoy pointing to the strict gun control in China and suggest that it would be terrible to live with the absence of basic freedoms such as free speech and the right to own a weapon for one's own protection.

Those in favor of gun control might point to the situation in a third world country where there are no controls. They might even say that it would be just awful to be victimized by roving, undisciplined gangs of young thugs, heavily armed and unrestricted by any laws, or for that matter, unlimited by the influence of any organized government.

It can be seen from just these two admittedly oversimplified, opposing, very biased selections that a convincing case can be made for any side of any issue by studying the data that are available and being just a little more efficient than the other fellow at finding the statistics that clearly tell things just the way they *should* be told.

A point to be made here is that for any controversial issue, from whether to continue life or to abort it or to prolong a suffering person's death or euthanize it, there can surely be found lots of arguments for the pro side and many also for the con. Each side will present its views with slogans and a few statistics designed to frustrate the opposition with powerful logic, hoping to persuade people to join them in support of their own particular cause.

It is also true for the issue of gun control. A spokesperson selecting statistics only from the con side of this issue can find enough evidence in support of his views against gun control to con everyone within earshot. It works the other way as well.

Those both for and against gun control seem to work at the extremes. Pro-gun lobbyists often see even the slightest restrictions on gun ownership and use as significant steps in the direction of ultimate confiscation of all weapons and a complete denial of the constitutionally guaranteed right to keep and bear arms. They hate the thought of being unarmed and also defenseless against the criminal element or the government under which they live.

On the other hand, many of those favoring regulation see a society out of control with gun violence that is escalating day by day as more and more people look to the gun as a means of resolving their conflicts, venting their frustrations and solving their problems.

Gun control advocates write aggressively about the juvenile attitudes of "gun nuts," "pro-gunners," "NRA propogandists" and "freedom freaks," etc., while others who want fewer restrictions on weapons call their opponents "gun-ban zealots," "their ilk," "spin doctors" or the "gun control crowd." Each side hates the biased arguments of the other side. Each is utterly appalled at how biased others can be when they have been influenced by those who are able to avoid truth that is so obvious.

Those who are authorized to make decisions based on statistical evidence find opposing factions flooding them with overwhelming amounts of conflicting data, confusing them with paranoid exaggerations, even threatening them with dire consequences. The decision-makers must be made to see the light and make their decisions accordingly.

Statisticians sometimes promote these extreme expressions with artfully contrived and biased data. Data that are intended to provide correlations between types of gun laws and increasing or decreasing rates of crime are used to reveal cause and effect, when actually, correlations alone provide no such thing. Correlations are relationship statistics. They are not appropriately used to establish cause and effect.

It is often said that there are liars, damned liars and statisticians. Today, most lobbyists hire statisticians to tell them how to do their damned lying. If you are against gun laws, you can read articles in magazines and newspapers that are against gun laws. You'll absorb the clever statistical arguments that convince you of the correctness of your point of view. Remember, there are dozens of statistics available to support any position on any controversial issue.

It works the other way too. The newspapers are filled with stories of tragic gun deaths. A few of them are represented in Chaper Two. Editorialists plead for protection from the gun. For the gun, by its very nature, it is said, becomes the instrument of violence. The writers' artfully chosen statistics show the carnage and provide the body count needed to convince others of the extent of the national tragedy.

They are self-fulfilling ideologies. The more time we spend reading reports filled with the statistics that support our own point of view, the more confident we become of the correctness of our own position.

Care is to be taken to avoid any serious consideration of the arguments of those who oppose that view, for those arguments are weak. They are without merit. No matter how logical they sound, they can be proven wrong by references to the statistics given by those of us who are better informed.

Do gun control laws work? Apparently, the answer to that question depends on whom you ask. Any representative of The Brady Campaign Against Gun Violence will show evidence that proves that they do. The NRA spokesperson will show you statistics that prove the reverse. Where does that leave the individual who would like a clear, honest answer to the question?

What interpretations should be drawn after a review of the conflicting arguments in favor and against the effectiveness of gun laws? The answer to this question is that we just don't know for sure. Nobody knows for sure. Those who claim that gun laws don't work point to their own selected statistics to show that they don't, but they don't know for sure. Some find statistics that support the opposite view, but they don't know for sure either. In the absence of any clear-cut consensus, each individual is left to his own devices and self-supporting biases as he struggles to convince himself that he is right and others who oppose him are wrong. Meanwhile, the killing goes on.

The Korean War took 54,260 American lives in three years in the early 1950s. The Vietnam War raged for over ten years in the late 1960s and early 1970s. There are now over 58,200 names on the memorial wall in Washington, D.C. known as the "Granite Wall."

In the past two years, gun deaths in the United States have totaled over 55,000! Would strong gun control laws and their enforcement reduce the number of deaths next year? Would the lives saved be worth the prices paid in curtailed freedoms of law-abiding citizens? The statisticians give us conflicting answers to these questions.

What do you think? You decide... Meanwhile, while you are trying to come up with an answer, eighty-two Americans are dying each day. Each day more children die. Your child could die. The killing goes on...

Chapter Four

The Armed Law-Abiding Citizen

Freedoms are not given up easily by most people unless it can be shown that their loss is in the interest of the society as a whole. People tend to stand very firm, both individually and collectively, fighting to preserve what they see as their God-given rights. They are very determined to convince others that their cause is the one that is just. They have every right to say what they think, to vote for what they believe in and to try to influence others to think as they do.

However, for every argument, there is a counter-argument, for every simple new solution, a variety of good reasons why it won't work. For every convincing proposal there is a strong counter-proposal, another possible way, the wrong way, disagreement as to which way. There are those who are quite convinced that they have the answer, those who know it's the wrong answer and a few who admit that they just don't know what the right answer *is*.

Inquisitive minds search for arguments that make sense. An orderly world is a more comfortable one in which to live, but as more and more arguments are considered, the quest for a simple straight line of truth yields to one that points in every conceivable direction. Sometimes, it goes around and around, enclosing the mind, isolating the ideas within from any other points of view.

Enter, the biases of everyone who argues for a particular point of view. Enter, the anger of those who don't agree, the zealots and their ilk, those idiots who can't be made to see the truth... So it is, in the realm of argumentation about so many social issues. Every person who promotes an argument is correct, that is, in his own opinion. The sense of frustration that results from being so right, yet unable to convince others that there is, for example, a basic freedom of reproductive choice, or conversely, that abortion is murder, or that the use of marijuana should be decriminalized, etc., is often overwhelming.

Those interested in gun control (or in its prevention) are among the most aggressive of all. Newspapers and magazines often contain editorials on this issue that are irrational, illogical and are filled very often with exaggerated emotionality. The arguments sound so appropriate and correct to those who agree with them, so biased and ludicrous to those who know better.

Let's look at some of the arguments proposed by those who tend to resist the move toward increased control over gun ownership and use. Consider, if you will, the concerns of the gun lobbyists. Consider also, some of the arguments of those who would oppose their point of view.

Criminals get away with an awful lot these days, from the simplest of crimes all the way to those most serious, even homicides. Even when caught, tried, found guilty and sentenced many appear on the streets again after only a short period of time, only to become repeat offenders. It's not unusual to find drivers still driving after ten or so convictions for drunk driving in some communities.

It seems at times to be almost impossible to protect others in the nation's cities from the drunk driver by seeing to it that he will not drive again. So ineffective is our present system of control, that it might be said that in the United States one is innocent until proven guilty *a number of times.*

Many criminals are guilty of crimes that involve the illegal use of a weapon. Some say that tighter regulation might result in fewer armed assaults, robberies and murders, because of the resultant limited availability of the gun itself. Still, others would ask, is it right to limit the availability of the gun to the good citizens who have no intention to use a weapon in the commission of any crime? Why not just punish the offenders?

Why punish law-abiding citizens by setting up laws that regulate their right to own and use arms? Why apply restrictions to the law-abiding?

Let's consider this same logic as we might apply it to the enforcement of traffic laws on the streets and highways of America. Consider the fact that only a small percentage of drivers are inclined to break the laws that regulate how a car is driven. Why then, should we setup laws that control the law-abiding drivers, thereby punishing them when they aren't the ones who really need to be controlled? Let's have laws that regulate the offenders, not the law-abiding drivers!

It should be seen easily that this logic is not going to hold, that laws that are considered fair and reasonable must be designed to apply to all persons equally. There's no magical way to know ahead of time who will be law-abiding and who will violate the law. There's no wisdom in the statement that only the criminal should be regulated. There is sense to be found in the point that all persons should be regulated, but only the drivers who have been found guilty of breaking the law should be punished.

It could be pointed out that most of the killing that is gun-related is done by someone who was not a criminal until the time that the trigger was pulled. It is more likely to be done by a citizen who was law-abiding before the tragic killing. As a result of anger, frustration and sometimes intent, many a law-abiding citizen has become a criminal. That criminal, then, should be punished.

It might be said that, as it is mandated in the Constitution, gun ownership and gun use should be well-regulated. It might even be argued that those who resist the enactment of appropriate laws that provide for that regulation are working to circumvent rather than facilitate the original intent of the founding fathers. Some of the anti-gun control organizations, however, seem to have as their major objective resistance to almost any form of regulation.

There are those who believe that a gun in the hands of a law-abiding citizen is the best available deterrent against crime. Homeowners should arm themselves, therefore, for the protection of their families. It is an argument that has been supported by the gun lobby for years. It sells guns. It may yield a sense of false security. It surely perpetuates the macho image of the gun-toting American hero. It can delude the gun owner into thinking that his children are safer if he is armed. The assumption may be false. Any gun that is purchased for the purpose of protecting one's family is many times more likely to bring injury or death to a member of that family than it is to protect it from any outside threat or from anyone with criminal intent. Most pro-gun lobbyists would, of course, be astonished at the stupidity of this assertion. "Look at the burglars who have been shot by law-abiding gun owners," they would say. However, burglaries usually occur when no one is home. Over 200,000 guns are stolen from homes across America every year. The gun bought to protect a family frequently becomes just a part of the loot, often ending up on the street, used in subsequent crime.

Burglars love homes with guns. Burglars love to steal guns. Criminals want more guns. Still, few gun enthusiasts would agree, as each envisions himself trapped in his home, hearing the breaking glass in the middle of the night, about to be victimized by an armed intruder who is going to steal his money and brutalize his wife. The gun is used to dispatch the bad guy.

It happens, but does it happen as often as the frequently reported scenario in which that same highly available gun is used either by intent or by accident to kill an innocent person, most likely one of the family members the gun was purchased to protect?

Many of the frequently cited cases support the gun-protection view. However, those who promote them are not inclined to note that the day that Arthur Boone shot and killed two assailants in Brooklyn, N.Y. (See Chapter Two), 110 other gun deaths occurred in America. Neighbors and family members were busy killing one another not out of defense but out of anger and by accident. The day Besse Jones protected herself by killing the teenager, 110 other gun-related deaths occurred, many of them deaths of family members that the guns were purchased to protect. An average of over 2,200 people per month died from bullets in the year 2002. Very few of those who died were criminals.

Try to remember the horror experienced by those watching the evening news on May 11, 1996 as they learned about the 110 people who died when flight *592* of Valuejet Airlines slammed into the mud and water of the Florida Everglades. Do you remember the screaming and wailing of the moms, dads and children of the victims, relatives who rushed to the airport to be advised that their loved-ones were on the DC-9 that had crashed amidst the snakes and alligators?

What a tragic loss of life! But, how much less tragic was the loss of an equivalent 108 lives that happened due to gunfire, sad losses that occurred *daily* in 1993 when the yearly total was *39,595?* Divide the total for the year by 365 to get the daily average. How much less tragic was each of the 108 *daily* deaths attributed to gunfire? Any newspaper of any large city in the United States is apt to have several stories per evening of gun deaths attributed to anger within a family, marital stress, divorce, child custody disagreements, road rage disputes, gang killings as well as accidental shootings that occur because the available gun was accessible to a child who showed it to his friends.

Only rarely, by comparison, is there a story in which a criminal is killed or captured by an intended victim. It happens, but not very often. "Newspapers don't report these cases as often," say the gun enthusiasts. "Perhaps, because they don't happen as often," say the gun control advocates.

One of the reasons, it is argued, that the gun serves as a deterrent to crime is the fact that the burglars, for example, are afraid of being shot by a well-armed citizen. He never knows if his potential victim is going to blow him away Thus, we are urged to assume that the armed law-abiding citizen helps to control crime even though he hasn't actually been involved in the act of shooting anyone.

It is argued further that criminals are afraid of the armed homeowner even more than of the police, the criminal being a little more afraid that the homeowner will shoot first, as the saying goes, then ask questions later. This argument is filled with alluring deception. It's, at best, a rationalization for those weapons owners who wish to assume some law enforcement responsibility for which they are untrained. Not only is the argument specious, it is quite dangerous as well.

It would be wise and prudent to recognize the limitations rather than the strengths of those who finish a sixteen-hour training course that permits them to carry a loaded, concealed weapon. It takes at least forty-five hours of lecture training to complete a college course in Sociology 101, but the successful completion of such a course does not qualify anyone as a sociologist. Four years of pre-med training gets a carefully selected student into medical school, but does not a physician make. Sixteen hours of training sessions on weapons hardly prepares anyone for the responsibility of controlling the criminal element.

Therein lies a significant danger not recognized to a sufficient extent by those who would promote laws that would actively encourage citizens to routinely carry concealed weapons as though it were their responsibility to protect not only their families, but society as a whole. It would be wise to note that as far as social policy is concerned, potential disaster could await members of any society that leaves the administration of justice to those least skilled.

Some go as far as to suggest that an effective method of criminal justice is involved when the criminal is shot by an armed citizen. Many an armed citizen, however, is serving time in prison for assuming that he alone was the correct one to be the administrator of that justice.

In a central Arizona community called Mesa, a man witnessed an armed robbery in progress and used his handgun to shoot at the two thugs as they escaped in a getaway car. His shots missed the car, but one bullet ricocheted off of the pavement and traveled across the street, hitting a woman who was sun-bathing poolside at a nearby motel. The bullet shattered the woman's lower jaw! Susan Dina died that day.

It can be seen, just from a rather cursory review of some of the most popular arguments in favor of gun ownership, that at first they can appear to be very logical and convincing. Whereas, after a closer look, all sorts of interesting implications and complications become evident. If you actually use a gun to protect yourself and you shoot someone, will the courts see that you were under the threat that you are claiming was present at the time? If you shoot the young men who threaten to hurt you unless you give them $5.00 on the subway, will a jury feel that you were justified in the use of a gun, in view of other options available to you at the time, notably, the ones you did not use? Are you sure that you are capable of making professional judgments when you are not a professional?

What if you misinterpret the intentions of a stranger in your own neighborhood, seeing him as a threat, when in actuality, he is not? What if he is simply at the wrong home, looking for the Halloween party?

Is it possible that you might end up in prison because you misinterpreted a situation and your untrained eyes saw more threat than was real?

"I'll have to take that chance," some will say, "rather than let the criminal hurt me or my kids."

Others regret what they have done. Many wish that they had relied on those trained to handle life and death situations instead of attempting to solve the problem themselves.

"I wish I had called the police before I tried to play hero," they say, as they pump iron with their fellow inmates, before their lockdown for the night.

Chapter Five

Predators at Bay

Any person seeing his family under threat will respond with any method needed to reduce or eliminate that threat. A look backward, after the excitement is all over, might find the law-abiding citizen seeing himself as one very fortunate to have had a gun at his disposal. "If I had not been armed, I could not have saved my kids," he might be saying. He could even be right.

But then, after returning home from work one evening, the same citizen might find his own son or daughter dead from a gunshot wound accidently inflicted by a friend being shown dad's gun. Or, the friend might be dead. What then, would the gun owner be saying? "If I had not been armed, i.e., not had a gun in my home, my son or daughter would not be dead. My neighbor's little girl would still be alive."

If only we could look far ahead, predicting the future, instead of just paying for the past. If only we could determine ahead of time what role the gun would have in our lives, a positive one of self -protection or a tragic one involving the injury or death of someone we love.

Surely, any law-abiding citizen who purchases a handgun for self protection has the best of intentions when it comes to what happens to his family. That person is convinced that he is doing the right thing in view of the large number of criminal types in the world who are themselves armed to the teeth. Why would the average citizen place himself at a clear disadvantage when facing the armed criminal? Maybe, he would be wise not to. Perhaps, he should always have a weapon at the ready in case a criminal should pose a threat to those he loves.

It would be great if he had a crystal ball that would tell him in advance if a criminal would threaten him or his family. If only he could know in advance if he would need a weapon, or, if unneeded, that the weapon wouldn't just lie around inviting family tragedy rather than family safety.

If only it would play out as it is shown to play out in the gun magazines. If only what he hopes will happen, would actually happen. If only the gun enthusiasts and lobbyists were certifiably correct in their assumption that armed families are more secure than those that are not.

They would have us believe it is so, but it may not be true. No one can be assured that owning a gun is the wise thing to do. That gun can kill a criminal. That same gun could destroy every dream its owner ever had. Unregulated in society, the gun leaves a trail of broken, even destroyed lives, at the same time saving some. It may be much more than a double-edged sword because it is so much more efficient in saving and throwing away human life.

Guns don't kill people, people kill people. Then why do we blame the gun for everything that happens? Why should we legislate against guns? The answer is that people kill one another *with* guns. People, then, are the objects of gun laws, not the guns themselves.

There are no laws against automobiles, but those who use them are well-regulated. The regulation is rightly placed. The law is correct when strong regulations govern the way people design, produce and use automobiles *and* guns.

It is often suggested that those who are intent on killing someone with a gun would only use something else if that gun were not available. So, as the argument goes, limiting the availability of guns is for naught. The killings would still occur. This is a clear rationalization, one that ignores the large number of deaths that wouldn't have occurred had there been no gun present.

Would Jennifer and her unborn baby have been killed on that Arizona freeway if the irate driver had not had a gun in his car? Would the child who found mommie's gun on the nightstand have killed his little sister with something else?

Would the young girl who died when the gun accidently fell from the car seat at the carwash be dead anyway, killed by some other means? Would the angry young men who were thrown out of the nightclub have returned to kill with other means if there had been no guns? Maybe, but most likely not.

No one would wish to be caught defenseless against those with evil intent. Wouldn't the enforcement of gun laws such as registration be more effective in controlling law-abiding citizens than it would be in controlling the criminal? After all, the criminal wouldn't be apt to obey the licensing laws, anyway. Criminals would still have their guns, it is feared, while registration would likely lead to confiscation, leaving the poor law-abiding citizen left in an emergency with only the option of dialing 911.

However, is it fair to ask if it is generally true that laws are unwise because some will tend to ignore them? Should we not have laws against driving recklessly because only the law-abiding will obey them, while the violators will not? Is it ill-advised to require all citizens to license their dogs, because some will not bother? Perhaps there should not be any laws against drunk driving, because so many ignore them.

These are legitimate concerns. How can the number of guns in the hands of criminals be reduced without in any way affecting the availability of protective weapons for those who wish only to keep their families safe? The answer is that they can't. Criminals get most of their guns from law-abiding citizens. They buy them legally or they steal them illegally. So, as more and more people purchase guns for protection, greater numbers of guns are made available as loot in robberies and burglaries. The more the gun is seen as the universal instrument of protection in a society, the more the gun becomes the instrument of threat. Many who are in favor of more control over the production, sale and use of guns feel that they are too easily obtained, too easily stolen and too easily used by too many people who have too much freedom to do with them as they please.

But, wait a minute! Does that mean that people shouldn't be allowed to buy them? Don't they have a right to own them? What does the Constitution say about this? Many folks remain convinced that the right to bear arms is a guaranteed constitutional right that is more important than the need to limit that right in any way in the interest of increased community security.

Are too many people deluding themselves with the erroneous assumption that they are safer when they own guns? Lots of Americans are convinced that they are keeping the predators at bay with their guns. However, the evil predators are not being kept at bay. They are everywhere and they are armed to the teeth with guns that are easily purchased from and stolen from law-abiding citizens who think they are helping to solve the problem by purchasing guns. Gun ownership, however, is not necessarily helping with this problem.

Burglars do not avoid burglarizing homes where there are guns. Instead, they wait until no one is home and then add the law-abiding gun owner's prized weapons to their loot. A prime motive for burglarizing homes is the hope that they will find guns. The very fact that gun shops across America need to be encased in bars on their windows and doors would indicate that even the gun shop owners know the criminals want the guns more than they fear the gun owner.

The gun manufacturer, the gun importer, the gunshop owner, the gun lobbyist and many gun enthusiasts would have the public believe that guns are the great deterrents that keep the evil element in society under control. They may be right. But then again, they may not be.

The reality is that the evil element in society is not under control. It might even be considered as being out of control. Americans today are not very safe. Guns are out of control. If guns made America safe, this most heavily armed citizenry in the world with its 220 million guns would find that its children were playing on the safest streets anywhere.

They are not.

Chapter Six

Who *Are* the Victims?

Citizens of the United States are frightened. It appears that they are going to get more so. They just do not feel as safe today as they did years ago. It's quite sad, but true. There's more danger for them in their homes. They are being asked to be more and more careful as they drive their automobiles, not only because they might get involved in an accident, but also because they might offend someone who is angry and armed.

Citizens of America are getting more and more afraid of going to work. Disgruntled employees are killing their employers and fellow employees. More and more, citizens of the big cities ride buses and metros in silence, concerned that they might be singled out by someone who is looking for a victim of the day.

Many people tend to get down on the criminal justice system these days for the simple, but frustrating reason that it seems to fail to do what it is supposed to do, which is to provide just punishment to the criminal. The public is seeing too much evidence of too little crime control. Criminals selling drugs are driving very expensive cars and burglars and robbers are getting back on the streets too quickly.

Murderers are having their penalties delayed for decades. Carjackers are living high, in more ways than one. In preceding generations, the criminal justice system was relied on to keep things under control. Today, the system is seen by many as one that cannot be counted on to keep others safe. Too many people are getting away with too much because the laws are not being adequately enforced. The police officer is not to be blamed for the problem. With rare exception, the typical cop is doing his job. He responds as quickly as he can, keeps his emotions under control as effectively as he can, respects the rights of others and arrests those who break the law. The men and women who wear a police uniform have incredibly difficult jobs to do and must risk their lives every day to do them. The job is becoming more and more difficult, however, because more and more people, at much younger ages, are challenging authority and more and more of them are carrying weapons.

To counter the influence of the greater number of young people who carry weapons, greater and greater numbers of young people and adults are carrying their own weapons. To counter the fact that the law enforcement system seems unable to curb the violence on the streets, more and more citizens are arming themselves to protect themselves from the violence on the streets. Well-intended as they are, too many of the gun owners are getting themselves involved in that same street violence, often trying to do what they are not trained to do. They tend to overreact, make poor judgments and complicate the work of the more qualified law enforcement officers.

It isn't likely that they provide significant help for the law enforcement officers when they try to go it alone, trying to solve problems of gun violence with more of their own gun violence. The greater the number of untrained gun owners in the United States, the greater is the problem of gun usage that is apt to cost more in tragedy than is gained in security.

A part of the problem is that the public is just as likely to shoot its foot as its foe. Accidents and the shooting of unintended victims may be more apt to occur than crime preventions. Husbands, wives and children are more apt to die than criminals. It is most unlikely, however, that any gun owner will be convinced of his increased vulnerability as a proud weapons owner. Surely, he would not make the mistakes that cost the lives of the innocent. Instead, he would protect his family from the bad guy.

Those who profit from the sale of arms have every reason to hope that the public will continue to increase safety with the purchase of more arms. They are sincere and are certainly within their rights to express their claim that crime will go down to the extent that criminals are afraid to break the law for fear that they will be shot by those who have weapons for self-defense. Some even claim that an armed society is apt to be a more polite society.

It may be an illusion. But then, it may not be. Representatives of the gun lobby, e.g., the National Rifle Association, could surely provide a significant number of statistics that "prove" that armed law-abiding citizens serve to deter crime. The leaders of the gun control organizations, e.g., The Brady Center To Prevent Gun Violence could show lots of statistical evidence that would "prove" that the reverse is true.

Pick up a gun magazine at your favorite discount store. Learn about the mini-gun, the miniature handgun being touted as one of the latest developments in the self-defense industry (actually, they have been available for years). Read the advertisements. "Easily concealed in purse or pocket." "You can defend yourself at work." "The most effective method of self-protection." "No one knows you are armed." Some of these guns are available for less than $60. "You can feel secure knowing that you can protect yourself."

These are messages readers are getting all over the country from some in the gun business. "Tip the odds in your favor," suggests one advertiser as a woman and two young children are shown standing near a nightstand table on which a bullet and a handgun are in clear view. Readers responding to this claim of increased safety can actually subject their own children to much greater threat, not less. Potentially deceptive ads like this can be as insidious as any cigarette advertisement designed to coerce the young.

In the next decade, millions of these miniature guns will be sold. They come in assorted shapes and sizes, designed to fire .22, .22L/R, .25 and .380 ammunition readily available everywhere along with the guns themselves. They come in ladies' styles, pearl styles, chrome styles and the traditional gunmetal blue, everything your self-defense requires except a trigger lock.

These guns appear to be innocuous enough. However, they pose an ever-increasing threat to the security of law-abiding citizens. Because as many as 200,000 guns are stolen every year in robberies and in burglaries, they often end up on the streets in great numbers in the hands of teen-agers and young adults inclined to protect themselves by shooting one another. The knowledge that there are hundreds of thousands of them in high riders, low riders and every size vehicle in-between on the nation's roadways makes for a dangerous society, not a safer one.

The fact that any co-worker or associate on any job in any business, any teen-ager in any classroom, any customer in a local restaurant, any driver on any street or highway, anyone on a bus or train, any shopper in any store or mall, etc., could be carrying a potentially lethal weapon at any time is frightening. Any one who is paying even the slightest attention to the number of deaths routinely occurring in the United States related to the gun should be appalled by this realization. The fact that gun lobbyists, while claiming a profound interest in the promotion of gun safety would actively campaign against any and all forms of regulation of this potential threat to public safety is disconcerting, to say the least. Apparently, either its leaders don't read the daily newspapers or they are unwilling to acknowledge the seriousness of hundreds of nightly shootings and the dozens of deaths that routinely occur, in spite of the fact that over the last decade an average of approximatley 30,000 lives per year have been lost to gunfire.

There are several questions that should be asked repeatedly of those who promote the gun-protection assumption of increased safety for armed law-abiding citizens. It would be interesting to know what percentage of the 28,663 American citizens who died from gunfire in the year 2000 were actually criminals. How many of those who died from bullets in 2000 were perfectly innocent people, fathers, mothers, sons and daughters who were shot by people using guns bought for personal protection? How many were killed by someone who was careless or who misinterpreted an imagined threat or lost control when a gun was readily available? How many times have those who died been the unintended victims of well-meaning, law-abiding gun owners?

How many *innocent* people were killed or maimed during the last decade by someone who was a law-abiding citizen just moments before the shots were fired? Among those armed law-abiding citizens who pur-chased the guns that killed innocent family members, relatives, neighbors or friends, how many attended funerals wishing that they had never bought the damned thing?

Chapter Seven

Regulations

On the morning of November 17, 1993, President Bill Clinton welcomed a grieving couple into the oval office at the White House. The couple had traveled from Japan to meet the president, hoping to discuss the tragic loss of their son who was shot to death in Baton Rouge, La., on Halloween night of the preceding year.

Masaichi and Meiko Hattori, parents of a sixteen year-old son, Yoshi, showed Clinton pictures of the boy as a child and pictures that the boy had taken of the president just one day before the shooting. A law-abiding homeowner killed Yoshi when he was alarmed by the costumed teenager who rang the doorbell at the wrong home on Halloween eve. Yoshi was going to a party.

The parents of Yoshi then presented the president with a quarter of a million signatures from Japanese citizens who appealed to him to end the gun violence in America. The boy's mother said that President Clinton, as indicated by the tears in his eyes, "felt sorrow for the tragedy that we had suffered" Approximately 37,700 gun deaths were recorded in America in 1992. The number for Japan was only several hundred.

How should the president have responded to those people, loving parents who sent their son to the United States as an exchange student from a country with relatively few guns, only to lose him to gun violence? It must have been a very difficult meeting for the president.

What should he have said to this couple? Should he have apologized for the fact that prior to that time it had been just about impossible to get any meaningful gun control laws through congress? Perhaps he should have apologized for the fact that there were over 220 million guns in citizen hands and that it was impossible to maintain any reasonable control over their use. Should he have apologized for the fact that it is becoming more and more dangerous for anyone from a foreign country to send his son or daughter to the United States because they may become the potential prey of the lawless in so many American communities?

Perhaps there's a more positive side to all of this. Maybe it's much too easy to exaggerate the tragic side of weapons use while avoiding any discussion of the positive role of guns in so many lives. After all, it would be a mistake to assume that all guns are purchased for the purpose of self-protection only or to quickly assume that all guns do is kill the innocent. They are frequently (mostly) purchased for entertainment purposes by the person who enjoys the out-of-doors and likes target shooting. They are used legally by hunters all over the world who seek food and enjoy the thrill of the hunt.

Guns are used in competitive sports. Marksmanship competition can be immensely exciting and challenging. Hobbyists collect weapons, spending endless hours searching in the gun publications and want ads to find additional sources. They treasure their highly valued acquisitions.

Gun shows are as popular today as autoramas and craft shows, if not more so. They provide weekend fun and entertainment for hundreds of thousands of citizens interested in adding to their collections. The collections tell them all about history, about peril and about the triumph of good over evil. Guns are valuable. They have served the nation well during times of war. They are relied upon by the police. Often they protect the innocent.

However, guns can also kill. As potential instruments of the deaths of so many citizens, their use should, at least to some extent, be regulated. Even the Second Amendment to the Constitution calls for arms to be well-regulated. Yet, many gun advocates, while relying on their own interpretation of that amendment as support for their individual right to bear arms, deny the wisdom of the founding fathers when it comes to regulation. Either they choose to support only that portion of the amendment that they favor or they insist that regulation does not mean gun control, as if there were another way to regulate arms besides enacting laws that seek to control.

Presently, tens of thousands of people, young and old, are routinely driving their cars on the nation's streets and highways with fully loaded revolvers and semi-automatic handguns on the seats, under the seats, in the glove compartments, or in holsters mounted on the doors. Bumper stickers are seen that boast, "THIS VEHICLE IS INSURED BY A .38."

Should it be legal for anyone, young or old, to be driving around town with a loaded gun in his car? Is it in the national interest for more and more vehicles to be occupied by armed drivers? Are the streets and highways made safer if more and more drivers are armed?

Representatives of the gun lobby should be encouraged to express their views on this issue. Should anyone old enough to be a licensed driver also be considered old enough to carry a gun in his car? Do those who offer seminars on the subject of ensuring citizen safety feel that there should be restrictions, whatever, on the right to drive a vehicle with a loaded gun within easy reach? If not, why not? If so, then what limitations should be in effect and how should those limitations be enforced? Would national legislation be appropriate for control over the extent to which armed drivers travel the public highways?

In November of 1993, the United States Senate did agree to ban the manufacture and sale of 19 types of assault style weapons. Included were the TEC-DC, AK-47, MAC-lO, the Baretta AR-70, Colt AR-15, the Styr Rifle and Streetsweeper shotguns. These weapons were said to be designed solely for military purposes and have on some occasions been used to kill groups of people. Designed in the Soviet Union in 1947, there are approximately 20 million AK-47s in circulation in the world today. A very large number of those weapons are in the United States.

SWD M-lO, M-ll and M-12 models are assault pistols designed to spray many bullets over a wide area in seconds. They were also banned under the Senate's proposal. They are manufactured based on the design of the fully automatic hand pistol, the Mac-lO. The assault weapons ban was finally signed into law by President Clinton in 1994.

Should the assault weapons ban be repealed? "Yes," says the NRA. Very few deaths occur as a result of the legal use of these weapons. Actually, this is quite correct. By far, most gun deaths that occur involve other types of weapons. About 30,000 tragic gun deaths per year occur as a result of gunfire from regular rifles, shotguns and handguns.

Why single out the assault weapon as the type to be banned when it is involved in so few killings? Maybe it is wise because of the multiple killings in Killeen, Texas in which 23 people were killed. Maybe it's because of the slaying of eight when a gunman terrorized members of a San Francisco law firm by spraying bullets with Tec-9 assault pistols. Maybe it's because of the five children killed and 29 persons wounded on a playground in Stockton, California by a sick, deranged gunman who used an AK-47 to fire 106 bullets at innocent kids over a period of just two minutes.

Handguns are the weapons used most frequently by criminals. Isn't it much more appropriate to regulate *them?* "Not so," says the NRA, lest the law-abiding citizen be deprived of his right to protect himself. Still convinced that handguns deter crime, the gun lobby tends to resist measures that will limit access and use of them by the law-abiding citizen.

Hoping to tap a heretofore under developed market, the industry is catering more and more to women, capitalizing on their fears, convincing them that guns are needed for their personal protection. Millions of small concealable guns will be sold in years to come, purchased by women who have become convinced that they are safer if they are carrying a gun or, at least, have one in their home or apartment. Whether or not they are, of course depends on whom you ask.

Of those measures involving gun control that can be seen as inhibiting the right to keep and bear arms, licensing is the one most likely to be fought by the gun lobby. Many of those who are against gun laws resist the idea of having any government agency aware of the weapons they possess. Some see a hoard of big brother-agents descending on them, invading their homes and absconding with their weapons, thereby denying them any protection against either government or the criminal. If the government is aware that they have them, it is complained, its agents can seek them out and confiscate them at will. "Look at what has happened in Canada," seems a frequent refrain.

The claimed likelihood of an abusive government that sweeps across the United States confiscating massive numbers of arms from those who own over 220 million of them would seem to be a bit of an overstatement. Those made so paranoid by this expectation are overreacting. The licensing of weapons does not mean the wholesale confiscation of the weapons of law-abiding citizens. Not now, not in the future.

A large part of the gun problem comes from the lack of a sense of responsibility shown by so many who own them. The requirement that guns be registered, it is argued, might encourage gun owners to pay closer attention to their disposition, seeing to it that they are not left in unlocked cars or left exposed on coffee tables or mounted on walls in homes. The result should be fewer weapons that are stolen.

Those who know that they will be held responsible for an inappropriate use of a gun registered in their name are more apt to see that their weapons are kept secure. "That's not necessarily true," say the gun enthusiasts. "Very likely," say those in favor of setting up a program that involves the licensing of gun owners.

No gun should be sold without a trigger lock by anyone who is a licensed dealer. "They won't use them," say many gun experts. "Why have another law?" "Because some owners would and some wouldn't. Those who would could save some lives by making sure that their children can't fire them," say the gun controllers. Would the saving of any lives at all make the cost of a trigger lock worth the price? What if it were the life of someone's daughter? If the objective of any gun regulation is to promote public safety, why would anyone be against such a law? Is the requirement for trigger locks just another step toward the arrival of the federal agents? If the representatives of the gun lobby would call for a strict requirement that trigger locks be packed with all guns sold, surely many lives would be saved. "Not necessarily," say the fellows who see the requirement as just another useless law.

Gun laws themselves should not be seen as good or bad, not any more than the guns themselves. In most instances, guns are used safely and intelligently. No laws should prohibit their use in this manner by persons mature enough to use them wisely. Reasonable regulations, however, need not interfere in any significant manner with the legitimate use of weapons for personal entertainment, sports, hunting activities or for the defense of self and family.

Reasonable regulations may, on the other hand, save lives by promoting a much greater sense of responsibility in those who decide to purchase weapons. If guns were registered, owners would know that their weapons could be traced right to them regardless of what they did with them, where they ended up or who owned them at a later time. A person owning a registered gun would be likely to show more interest in the integrity of its next owner. "Not necessarily," say the fellows who are cringing at the thought of registration. "What if it is stolen? Why should I be held responsible for it, then?" "Because it's your responsibility to see that it *isn't* stolen," say the ones in favor of licensing.

Is the problem of gun violence serious enough so that law-abiding citizens would be willing to see an increase in the overall number and kinds of restrictions placed on the availability and use of weapons by *all* persons? National polls seem to indicate so. With a high youth crime rate marked by gang warfare, carjackings, drive-by shootings and armed robberies, the average citizen is beginning to realize that there are too many guns in the hands of too many people who are inclined to use them with too much freedom.

Contrary to the stated beliefs of many gun lobbyists, reasonable gun regulation can serve as an appropriate part of the solution to the problem of national violence. Gun control will not stop violence any more than drunk driving laws will stop people from drinking and driving. Many believe however, that well enforced national, state and local legislation that regulates the production, possession and use of guns can help reduce some of the violence, lessening the severity of the problem.

Why should the weapons industry be uniquely exempted from government regulation of its products while almost all other industries are subjected to rules that control the design, production and use of their consumer products? If the automotive industry must comply with strict requirements for safety with mandatory installation of air bags, regulation of bumper strength and strict requirements for limitations of noxious emissions, why are there so few government regulated requirements for safety with the production of guns?

In the year 2008 there was not a single death that occurred in any accident related to the well-regulated American commercial aviation industry. Yet, those who produce aircraft for commercial aviation must respond to comprehensive federal regulations with regard to the design, production and maintenance of their products. Why are there no similar legal requirements for the design and production of weapons that were involved in an estimated 29,000 deaths of American citizens during that same year?

For the protection of the American consumer, there is a Code of Federal Regulations (CFR) that involves laws that affect products and services. An annual cumulative codification of rules and regulations is published yearly in the Federal Register. The complete CFR contains 50 titles and approximately 900 volumes. Included are the areas of Agriculture and its products, Animals and related products, Aeronautics and Space, Banks and Banking, Commodity and Securities Exchanges, Commercial Practices, Food and Drugs, Housing and Urban Development, Parks, Forests and Public Property, Protection of the Environment, Public Health, Public Welfare, Communications, Transportation, Wildlife and Fisheries, to name just a few. The long list of regulating agencies seems endless. While that very long list does also include Alcohol, Tobacco Products and Firearms, very few regulations apply to the design, production and distribution of the products of the gun industry. Why?

The Food and Drug Administration regulates the meat industry, the food processing industry, product labeling and the pharmaceutical industry, etc. The Consumer Product Safety Commission can recall defective toy guns, but not defective *real* guns! What is it about the gun industry that should make its products exempt from federally mandated safety regulations when it comes to their design and manufacture?

If thousands of lives were lost each year in aircraft-related accidents across America, would the public be likely to heed arguments from the

CEOs and lobbyists in the airplane industry when they claimed that no further regulation was needed? Would the public be inclined to agree with the lobbyists who say that all that is needed is stronger enforcement of existing laws? Or would they demand greater regulation in the interest of increased public safety?

Individual citizens might ask themselves if they think that consumer products should be regulated at all. Some feel that they should be regulated, but not by the federal government. Maybe only state regulations should apply, even though they would tend to be inconsistent from state to state. Some, lacking any faith in the integrity of politicians in general, would prefer that the producers of consumer products be left alone, encouraged only to regulate themselves.

Very conservative persons suggest that the federal government has no business regulating the design, production and distribution of weapons. Any step taken to get greater control over guns is seen as a progressive move toward infringement.

Why not let the gun manuflicturers police themselves, letting the competition and the preferences of the consumer be the deciding factors as to how guns are designed, manufactured and distributed?

The problem with this approach is that self-regulation is apt to be restrained by many companies when it is in conflict with the interest of CEOs in a positive bottom line report to the stockholders who invest for profit. It would be wise for citizens to ask themselves if they would rather travel on commercial airplanes that have been designed, produced and maintained under self-regulatory practices by the manufacturers and the airline companies themselves or by a government agency (the FAA) that is not directly affected by monetary considerations.

Would the citizen prefer to leave regulation of the initial development, production and release of medications for public use to the drug companies themselves, rather than to a federal agency (the FDA) that is not directly sensitive to the profit motive? Should the meat packing companies be alone in regulating the quality of the meats that reach the family dinner table?

What is it about the products of the weapons industry that should result in their design, production and distribution being exclusively exempted from most government regulation? Perhaps it's because there is less potential threat to the security of the public in the use of these products. Perhaps few deaths and injuries occur that are related to the use and abuse of these products.

Perhaps...

Chapter Eight

Courting Gun Rights

"Because the Second Amendment does not confer an individual right to own or possess arms, we affirm the dismissal of all claims brought pursuant to that constitutional provision."

"Because we hold that the Second Amendment does not provide any individual right to own or possess guns or other firearms, plaintiffs lack standing to challenge that opinion."

United States Court Of Appeals Opinion - For the Ninth Circuit

Filed December 5, 2002 In the Case of Silveira V. LockyerNo. 01-*15098* D.C. No. CV-00-00411-WBS

For as long as can be remembered, the representatives of the National Rifle Association have touted the concept of the constitutionally protected right of individuals to keep and bear arms. Dependably, in television interviews, printed editorials, magazine articles and book presentations, the enactment of many new gun laws was reported as a potential violation of the Second Amendment which guaranteed that the law-abiding citizen's constitutional right to keep and bear arms could not be infringed.

Polls have shown that as many as 70% of the American people believe that the Second Amendment assures the right for any individual to own a gun. Representatives of the gun lobby have sold this concept so hard for so long that hardly anyone would dare to challenge it. A major guiding principle for the philosophy and the agenda of the NRA is that citizens' constitutional rights cannot be denied, especially those involving the ownership of a gun.

The 2002 opinion stated in the Ninth District Court case of *Silveira v. Lockyer,* however, denies that such a right is conferred to individuals by the Second Amendment. As the largest of the district circuit courts, it is the Ninth Court, with its constituancy of fifty-six million citizens that sends the sweeping message that challenges one of the major tenets of the gun lobby, namely that gun rights for individuals are established in the Bill of Rights by the Second Amendment.

Excessively buoyed by an opinion released (Nov. 2001) in the case of *U S. A. v. Emerson* that supported individual rights, several writers hailed that opinion as if it offered a resolution of the issue of gun rights in favor of the gun advocates. Thus they provided the opinion that those who supported the collective (militia only) concept rather than the individual rights model were at last shown to be in error.

Almost gloating over the prospect of successfully proving their case in the courts those writers applauded the wisdom of Fifth Circuit Senior Judge William L. Garwood who endorsed the individual rights concept.

Wrote Judge Garwood in a summary statement, "It appears clear that *the people,* as used in the Constitution, including the Second Amendment, refers to *individual* Americans (italics added)." This verification of the coveted conviction of members of the gun lobby that individuals, not just militiamen, were guaranteed the right to keep and bear arms by the Second Amendment came as welcome "proof," indeed. At last, the court had settled the issue of collective vs. individual rights and had done so in favor of the position held by the gun lobby for the last fifty years. The important principle of a constitutionally guaranteed right for any individual citizen to keep and bear arms, fervently defended by the gun lobby, had emerged fully intact. Those who resisted that principle were clearly wrong.

Only a year later, however, the largest district court in the land denied that very principle. Unless the opinion in *Silveira v. Lockyer* is overturned by the full court or by the United States Supreme Court, gun lobbyists will have to accept the fact that their claim of any *individual* constitutional right to keep and bear arms is unsubstantiated. In December of 2003, the U. S. Supreme Court decided not to hear a challenge to California's assault weapons ban. In doing so, they upheld a lower court's opinion that the right to bear arms applies only in connection with a state militia. If, in the opinion of the gun lobbyists, what is important is that the underlying principle of individual gun rights be upheld by the courts, the lobbyists must be stunned by this significant setback. It is clear that the courts, *including the Supreme Court,* do not see it their way.

Meanwhile, the gun lobby uses the questionable concept of individual constitutional gun rights to support an agenda that resists the ban on assault weapons and attempts to limit the rights of gunshot victims to get retribution in the courts. One such argument against the assault weapons ban is reasonable and well-considered. It is frequently (and rightly) pointed out that assault weapons account for only a small percentage of the homicides in America. Yet, gun control advocates were able to get President Clinton to sign the ban in 1994. The bill expired ten years later in 2004. As was expected, the gun rights activists let the bill die quietly, while the gun controllers proposed legislation in both the U.S.House of Representatives and the U. S. Senate not only to extend the bill, but to tighten its provisions as well. Should the bill have been allowed to die or should it have been reenacted in expanded form? It depends on whom you ask.

Should gunshot victims have the right to sue gun manufacturers or distributors if they feel that they should be held liable for their negligence? Or, should there be a special immunity from such suits to avoid frivolous threat to the integrity of the weapons industry? To what legal extent is a gun manufacturer or gun distributor liable for the use of a weapon that has been used in an unlawful act?

Gun advocates have a strong argument when they plead for immunity from lawsuits threatened simply because they produced or sold the weapon that killed or injured someone. "After all," it is argued, "if a kid steals a Chevy and runs someone down with it, is General Motors at fault?" If someone falls off of a Harley-Davidson motorcycle, should the company be held accountable? Still, what if the car or motorcycle had a design flaw that could have contributed to the death or injury of someone? Should the company then be immune from litigation that might result in compensation for the victim? What if a distributor knowingly sells guns to criminals?

Unfortunately, there are some unscrupulous weapons distributors who are involved in supplying criminals with guns. Many lawsuits are being filed that can result in compensation to victims from gun dealers and distributors who have been involved in this process. The gun industry, however, is against these lawsuits, even to the extent of gaining passage of an "immunity" bill (H.R.1036) that is designed to protect gun manufacturers, dealers and distributors from suits that claim negligence on the part of these suppliers. Passage of a companion bill in the U. S. Senate *(S.659)* is likely as well, but may be prevented from passage by a potential filibuster endorsed by the Brady Center for the Prevention of Gun Violence, an organization that represents many victims who have brought these suits.

Most senators, congressmen and congresswomen wouldn't think of granting immunity to the auto industry, the airlines or even the toy manufacturers. But, guns? Should the families of the victims of the "Beltway" snipers in Washington, D. C. be denied the right to sue the company that was allegedly negligent in supplying the XM-15 Bushmaster rifle that was used in killing twelve people in the fall of 2002? Is it reasonable to deny the survivors their day in court? Apparently, the answer depends on whom you ask.

Should the Bureau of Alcohol, Tobacco and Firearms (ATF) be able to require inventory controls for gun dealers? Should records of background checks from gun sales be immediately destroyed after the sales? The NRA claims that multiple firings of a rifle will alter the "fingerprint" of a weapon, yet the same weapon was shown to have been involved in eight of the twelve killings in the "Beltway" case. Would a "fingerprinting" system for guns be useful for law enforcement? It depends on whom you ask.

Should "kitchen-table" dealers be licensed to sell guns or should those licenses be denied? Should those licensed to carry concealed handguns be allowed to carry them into public schools, churches, any restaurants, parks and grocery stores at any time? Would the average American citizen be made to feel safer as he or she drove to work, did the routine shopping, attended church services, went to a baseball or a football game or took the family on a picnic if it were known that other persons who were in attendance were carrying concealed guns? Again, the answers to all of these questions depend on whom you ask.

Chapter Nine

The Right to Keep and Bear Arms

Do people have the right to keep and bear arms as is stated in the Second Amendment to the United States Constitution? Why all of the present day controversy over this issue? Don't citizens have the right to protect themselves and doesn't this imply the right to possess firearms? What was the intent of the founding fathers with regard to this issue when they formulated the second of the ten amendments that became known as the Bill of Rights? The date of ratification was December 15, 1791.

The Second Amendment reads as follows:

"A well-regulated Militia, being necessary to the **security** *of a free State, the right of the people to keep and bear arms, shall not be infringed."*

The amendment attracted very little judicial or scholarly attention for over a century and a half with little concern over the founders' intended definition of the term "militia," or precisely what "people" were relegated the right to keep and bear arms. In recent years, as a result of increasing problems with gun violence, the right to keep and bear arms has become a matter of intense controversy, subject to a variety of interpretations of the amendment.

Those trying to gain greater control over guns in America see the amendment as limited in meaning, concerned only with the establishment of the state militias as protection against a potentially tyrannical federal government and having nothing to do with the establishment of rights for individuals.

Those who champion the individual rights interpretation tend to use the Second Amendment as a source of undeniable support for the right of people to keep and bear arms. There seems to be no middle ground on the issue, proponents from each side persistently defend their own interpretation of the founders' intent.

The words of Thomas Jefferson are echoed by representatives of the gun lobby. "No free man shall ever be debarred the use of arms." How could the argument for an individual right to own a gun be stated more directly than that? Yet, many see the pronouncement by Jefferson only as argumentative discourse having nothing to do with an amendment that was then intended primarily to keep the federal government from restricting the right of the states to form their own militias.

So, the debate rages on, each side bombarding the other with imaginative statistics, slogans and even bumper stickers trying to undercut the narrative of the uninformed opposition. However entertaining and informative that it is, dazzling to the eye as are all of the charts, graphs and advertisements, they offer little to resolve the conflict. Nothing is offered that effectively settles the issue of whether the Second Amendment was intended by the founding fathers as one that protects the rights of the states to form militias or the right of *individuals* to keep and bear arms.

Fortunately, the Constitution itself provides a method, i.e., a modus operandi, for resolving troubling disagreements between parties when constitutional issues are involved. Public discourse set aside, Article III of the United States Constitution provides for the adjudication of disputed claims by the consigned authority of the Supreme Court. Section 1 reads:

"The Judicial Power of the United States shall be vested in one Supreme Court and in such inferior Courts as the Congress may from time to time ordain and establish. The Supreme Court shall have appellate jurisdiction, both as to Law and Fact, with such Exceptions, and under such Regulations as the Congress shall make."

So, it is to the Supreme Court and the Circuit Courts inferior to it that we must turn in order to get clarification as to what the Second Amendment means by law. Interpretations that find support in case law before the Courts are accepted as indicative of the intent of the founders of the Constitution.

The nine members of the Supreme Court have the ultimate authority to decide constitutional issues. Often, however, the issues do not reach the Supreme Court and are decided by members of the Circuit Courts. Only a very small percentage of the cases reviewed at the Circuit Court level are appealed all the way to the Supreme Court.

As an example of the way Supreme Court decisions supersede the public discourse, one might note the aggressive argumentation that took place on the abortion issue during the 60s. Representatives of each side, pro-life and pro-choice quoted learned historians, philosophers, the Pope and the Bible. Medical specialists were quoted. Legal scholars were quoted. In the end, however, it took the Supreme Court in 1973 to settle the issue (to the extent that it is settled today) and thus to formulate law with Roe v. Wade. As generally stated, the Court supported the mother's right to choose an abortion. It appears today that it will take a Supreme Court decision to settle the issue of Second Amendment collective (militia) vs. individual gun rights also, in view of the fact that recent Circuit Court reviews have resulted in conflicting opinions on the issue.

It seems unlikely that Federal District Courts would provide opinions on any constitutional issue that could be in direct conflict with one another, but in two cases reviewed as recently as 2001 and 2002, that's precisely what happened. On the issue of gun rights, individual or collective, the Fifth Federal Circuit Court (Louisiana, Mississippi and Texas) decided in favor of individual rights in November of 2001 in the case of *U. S. A. v. Emerson,* (270 F.3d 203 227). The Ninth Federal Circuit Court (Alaska, Arizona, California, Hawaii, Idaho, Montana, Nevada, Oregon and Washington) decided in favor of collective rights in December of 2002 in the case of *Silveira v. Lockyer* (01 -15098 D.C. No. CV - 00-00411-WBS).

Is it any wonder that the public is confused? Is it any wonder that even United States Attorney General John Ashcroft had some trouble deciding how to advise the nation's prosecuting attorneys on the issue of gun rights? If the courts can't agree, then how are legal authorities, let alone the American citizens, to know the extent of personal gun rights under the law?

Perhaps a review of a few significant cases on the issue of gun rights, beginnning in 1939, will be useful. The Supreme Court has not often reviewed the issue, yet, one case in that year and later circuit court cases have resulted in a case law trend that leans toward the acceptance of Second Amendment rights as applied *only* to the establishment of state militias and not to the right of individuals to bear arms. Or, stated in a different way, individuals were not supported in their claims that the Second Amendment guaranteed the right to bear arms if their activities were not related to their membership in an organized militia.

In 1939, in the case of *United States v. Miller* (307 U.S. 174, 1939), the Court addressed the individual rights position wherein a criminal defendant issued a Second Amendment challenge to a federal gun control law that prohibited the transport of sawed-off shotguns in interstate commerce. The Court rejected the challenge. The *Miller* Court concluded *"In the absence of any evidence to show that possession or use of a shotgun having a barrel of less than eighteen inches in length at this time has some reasonable relationship to the preservation or efficiency of a well-regulated militia, we cannot say that the SecondAmendment guarantees the right to keep and bear such an instrument."*

Thus, in *Miller,* the Supreme Court decided that because a weapon was not suitable for use in the militia, its possession was not protected by the Second Amendment. The Court opinion negates the protection of possession of only certain kinds of weapons, however, and is said not to apply any general rule. What *Miller* does strongly imply is that the Supreme Court rejects the Second Amendment's traditional *individual* rights view.

In *Lewis v. United States* (445 U.S. *55,65* n 8, 1980), the *Miller* holding was characterized in the following manner: *"The Second Amendment guarantees no right to keep and bear a firearm that does not have some reasonable relationship to the preservation or efficiency of a well-regulated militia." Lewis* does serve to reinforce the strong implication in *Miller* that the Court rejects the concept of any *individual* Second Amendment rights.

Certainly, this view is not accepted by everyone, either in or outside of the courts. Members of the gun lobby disagree vehemently, preferring to define the "people" in the Second Amendment as applied to all able-bodied American citizens who are law-abiding and not affected by any criminal, mental or emotional exclusion by law.

In dozens of cases appealed to the inferior (District) courts through the last half of the twentieth century, the decisions have rather consistently affirmed the collective (militia only) view as opposed to that of individual rights. This body of case law stands in suppport of *Miller* in its implication that the Second Amendment does not guarantee any *individual* rights.

Still, this traditional view was vigorously challenged as recently as in November, 2001 before justices of the Fifth Federal District Appeals Court in a scholarly, comprehensive 84-page opinion that supports the individual rights point of view.

In *U.S.A. v. Emerson,* a case is cited in which the Grand Jury for the Northern District of Texas returned an indictment against Dr. Timothy Joe Emerson alleging that Emerson was in unlawful possession of a firearm, a Baretta pistol, while subject to a temporary injunction prohibiting such possession by a judge (Sutton) in the 119th District Court of Tom Green County, Texas.

Emerson moved to have the indictment dismissed asserting that his Second Amendment rights were being violated. The Fifth District Court agreed. An informative, scholarly analysis of several interpretations of the Second Amendment appears as part of the opinion in *Emerson: "In the last few decades, courts and commentators have offered what may fairly be characterized as three different basic interpretations of the Second Amendment. The first is that the Second Amendment does not apply to individuals; rather, it merely recognizes the right of a state to arm its militia. This "states' rights" or "collective rights" interpretation of the Second Amendment has been embraced by our sister circuits.*

Proponents of the next model admit that the Second Amendment recognizes some limited species of individualized right. However, this supposedly "individual"right to bear arms can only be exercised by members of a functioning, organized state militia who bear arms while and as a part of actively participating in the organized militia's activities. The individual right to keep and bear arms only applies to members of such a militia.

The third model is simply that the Second Amendment recognizes the right of individuals to keep and bear arms. This is the view advanced by Emerson and adopted by the district court. None of our sister circuits has ever subscribed to this model, known by the commentators as the individual rights model or the standard model. The individual rights view has enjoyed considerable academic endorsement, especially in the last two decades."

The position of the Fifth Circuit is later summarized by the following statement: *"In undertaking this analysis, we are mindful that almost all of our sister circuits have rejected any individual rights view of the Second Amendment. However, it respectfully appears to us that all or almost all of these opinions seem to have done so either on the erroneous assumption that Miller resolved that issue or without sufficient articulated examination of the history and text of the Second Amendment."*

Representatives of the gun lobby have feasted on the opinion stated in *Emerson* as it supports what they have always known, namely, that the founding fathers meant for the right to keep and bear arms to apply to all citizens, even those in no way affiliated with an organized militia. "People" means *all* of the people, not just those in state militias.

The justices of the Fifth Circuit Court had given the gun industry representatives and the leaders of the NRA the decision they wanted. It follows, therefore, that any law that in any way limits or restricts the constitutionally guaranteed right for any individual law-abiding citizen to own a gun is ill-advised. Surely, if you have the United States Constitution behind you, you are quite justified if you resist any regulation that might serve to reduce the expression of your rights.

Anyone who tries to ban assault weapons is denying you a right that you have under the Constitution. Anyone who tries to prevent you from carrying a concealed weapon is trying to deny you your right to do so in spite of the fact that the Constitution guarantees your right to keep and bear arms. The gun lobbyist sees the issue in that way and tries to prevent the enactment of any legislation that might infringe on gun rights. Were the justices of the Fifth District Court correct in supporting a Constitutional basis for *individual* gun rights? "Oh yes," said the gun lobbyists.

There wasn't any way for the pro-gun activists to anticipate a subsequent court decision, one that shocked them back to a more realistic picture with regards to this constitutional issue. It came from the Ninth Circuit Court of Appeals (viewed by many as the second highest Court in the land) and it held an opposing view. The December, 2002 decision in the case of *Silveira v. Lockyer* denied any Second Amendment guarantee of the right to own or bear arms. The Court stated as follows: *"Because the Second Amendment does not confer an individual right to own or possess arms, we affirm the dismissal of all claims brought pursuant to that Constitutional provision* This decision is seen as a setback for the *NRA*.

In 1989, there was a random shooting at the Cleveland Elementary School in Stockton, California. An individual armed with an AK-47 semiautomatic weapon opened fire on the school yard where 300 pupils were at morning recess. Five children, aged six to nine, were killed. One teacher and 29 other children were wounded. The California Assembly, meeting soon afterward, enacted a response to the shooting. It was then named the Roberti-Roos Assault Weapons Control Act ("the AWCA"), the first legislative restriction on assault weapons in the nation. It eventually served as a model for a quite similar federal statute enacted in 1994.

The AWCA made it a felony offense to manufacture, possess, sell, transfer or import into the state certain semi-automatic weapons without a permit. In 1999, 'the state legislature amended the AWCA in order to broaden its coverage. Only one month after the new amendments took effect, plaintiffs who owned assault weapons challenged the AWCA requirements that they register, relinquish or render inoperable their assault weapons claiming that their Second Amendment rights were being violated. In *Silveira,* that challenge is dismissed. *"Our court, like every other court of appeals to reach the issue except the Fifth Circuit, has interpreted the Miller opinion as rejecting the individual rights view."*

Jamie Lucier, Ph.D.

The December, 2002 Ninth Circuit opinion in *Silveira* supports the collective rights model. *"Appellants argue that the Caltfornia Assault Weapons ControlAct and its 1999 revisions violate their SecondAmendment rights. We unequivocally reject this contention. We conclude that although the text and structure of the amendment, standing alone, do not conclusively resolve the question of its meaning, when we give the text its most plausible reading and consider the amendment in light of its historical context and circumstances surrounding its enactment we are compelled to reaffirm the collective rights view we adopted in Hickman v. Block (81 F.3d 98, Ninth Cir. 1996): The amendment protects the peoples' right to maintain an effective militia, and does not establish an individual right to own or possess firearms for personal or other use. This conclusion is reinforced in part by Miller's implicit rejection of the traditional individual rights position. Because we contend that the SecondAmendment does not provide an individual right to own or possess guns or other frearms. plaintiffs lack standing to challenge the opinion."*

The Supreme Court could have reversed the more recent *Silveira v. Lockyer* opinion, thereby affirming the individual rights view as would be preferred by the gun lobby. Or, its members could have upheld an opinion in favor of the collective view. As a third option, the Court could have just refused to review the issue, leaving intact the opinion that denies any individual rights granted by the Second Amendment.

The last of these options was the one chosen by the Court. In June of 2008, however, the issue of collective vs. individual right to bear arms was considered by the U.S. Supreme Court which affirmed an individual right.*

* A detailed analysis of the Court's opinion in District of Columbia v. Heller appears as the last chapter in this book.

Chapter Ten

Now, Wait a Minute...

By now it can be seen that the answer to the question of individual gun rights depends on whom you ask. Actually, there are two questions involved. One is whether or not there is any such thing as an individual right and the other is whether or not that right, if it does exist, is derived from the wording of the Second Amendment to the United States Constitution.

In earlier chapters, the issue of Second Amendment rights was addressed. The most relevant of the court opinions was from the Nmth Circuit Court of Appeals. It stated in *Silveira v. Lockyer* in December of 2002 that the Second Amendment does not confer any individual right to own or possess arms. The decision could have been reversed by the same court. It could have been reversed by the justices of the United States Supreme Court. They refused to do so. Some things had become quite clear as a result of that circuit court opinion:

1. The self-assured claim by representatives of the National Rifle Association that the Constitution provides a guaranteed right for individuals to own arms was, at best, suspect at that time.

2. Attorney General John Ashcroft's change in policy in 2001 in a memo to federal prosecutors to expand the intended scope of the Second

Amendment from a collective right to an individual right was subject to question.

3. The opinion in *Emerson* (2001) of the Fifth District Court in favor of an individual right was very unique because it wasn't supported traditionally by other courts.

4. The powerful Ninth Circuit Court opinion expressly denied the conferment of any *individual* right to own or possess arms derived from the Second Amendment.

5. An eleven-member "en banc" panel of the judges from the Ninth Circuit Court could overturn the *Silveira v Lockyer* opinion that was based on the opinions of only three of the judges. Unless and until that happens or until the United States Supreme Court over turns that opinion, representatives of the gun lobby are limited in their claim of any constitutional support for the right of *individuals* to keep and bear arms.

In their written opinion in *Silveira v Lockyer* the justices quoted a significant former justice of the Supreme Court who, when interviewed, stated that the individual rights view was "one of the greatest pieces of fraud, I repeat the word 'fraud' on the American public by special interest groups that I've ever seen in my lifetime. The real purpose of the Second Amendment was to ensure that the state armies - the militia - would be maintained for the defense of the state. The very language of the Second Amendment refutes any argument that it was intended to guarantee every citizen an unfettered right to any kind of weapon he or she desires."

The justice was none other than the Honorable Warren E. Burger, the former Chief Justice of the United States Supreme Court, who was appointed by the very conservative President Richard M. Nixon in 1969. The interview was conducted in 1993, years after Burger's retirement from the Court in 1986. Burger had served as the Supreme Court Chief Justice for 17 years. In fairness, it should be noted that the justices in *Silveira* didn't share in Justice Burger's view that the Second Amendment enthusiasts were guilty of fraud, but they stated, "we do generally agree with his statements regarding the amendment's purpose and scope."

If Justice Burger was correct in his assessment, the NRA's scholars have been misrepresenting that purpose and scope for over five decades.

Every time a gun-activist goes on TV and stands in defense of a constitutional right for an individual to bear arms, that person is defending a right that may not exist. The often repeated claim that constitutional rights are being violated by those who promote more restrictive gun laws can be quite misleading. In light of the firm ruling in *Silveira v. Lockyer,* it may be appropriate to back away from that claim.

But, wait a minute! Does that really mean that the American citizen has no right to keep and bear arms? Is that what the court is saying - that no citizen has an individual right to own a weapon? The answer to that question is an unequivocal "No." The court is not denying the right of citizens to own or possess a firearm. The Ninth Circuit Court had oniy decided that the right is not protected *by the Second Amendment.* Note however, that in 2008, the Supreme Court did affirm an *individual* right. Does the citizen have the right to own a gun, keep a gun in his or her home, go hunting with a gun, engage in sporting activities with a gun or protect himself or herself with a gun? The answer is "Yes," an unequivocal "Yes." Assuming that person to be a law-abiding citizen, unaffected by threatening mental instability or criminal intent, there is no basis for denying access to any gun deemed legal to own. Generally, handguns, rifles and shotguns are legal to own, store, shoot or trade without any threat of penalty as long as those activities are engaged in accordance with existing laws.

Even if its linkage to the Second Amendment is successfully challenged, the right to own a gun remains intact. It should remain so. That right exists even without any Second Amendment linkage simply because any citizen has a right to own anything that is not illegal to own. In that sense, the right to own a gun comes from the same consideration as the right to own, say, a television set or a waterbed.

Gun advocates tend to find this interpretation unsettling in light of the history and tradition connected to gun ownership in America. Some even claim "sacred" rights, as though they have been conferred by a "higher order." Of course, it's impossible to find proof of this, but then, there is no proof that these rights don't exist either. It depends on whom you ask.

Certainly, no law-abiding gun owner wants to feel as if he or she is a danger to society or that he or she needs to be set apart from others as an antisocial extremist bent on intimidating others. They simply want to enjoy their guns as tools for their entertainment, as collectable, valued works of precision craftsmanship, as weapons used in supervised competitive sports activities and as instruments available for personal protection if and when they are needed.

They love to hunt deer, doves and ducks. They love the out-of-doors, the test of their marksmanship skills and the fun they have as they plink away at clay pigeons, paper targets and tin cans. They love the sound of rifle fire echoing through a canyon and the feel and sound of a freshly cleaned weapon with bolt, slide or pump action that works ever so smoothly and efficiently.

There is nothing wrong with this. True, guns *can* be used in evil ways, but they are not usually used that way. The typical law-abiding gun owner does not wish to be branded as an antisocial person because of the relatively small percentage of gun owners who use them in aggressive violation of the law. Conversely, those who are concerned about the many tragic deaths that *do* occur by gunfire in America, either by intent or accident, do not wish to be thought of as being less patriotic, less concerned about individual human rights or less courageous in the need to protect their families.

A commitment to more and better regulation of the use of weapons in America may be in the interest of increased public safety. A reduction in the number of gun-related deaths is surely an honorable objective. So, also, is determined resistance by the gun lobby to any unneeded reduction in citizens' rights, including the right to bear arms.

Chapter Eleven

Handgun Protection?

Is it in your interest to purchase a gun for your own protection and the security of your family? Considering the danger that is everywhere, a firearm, handy when you need it, could save your life and the lives of the ones you love. Sometimes, however, gun ownership turns into tragedy. Knowing that some good people as well as the bad can get shot with guns, should most well-meaning homeowners, apartment dwellers, vacationers, businessmen and businesswomen, teachers and drivers be encouraged to carry a gun for personal protection?

There are lots of ways to search for a good answer to that question. One way is to ask the guy who sells them. His answers will appear to make good sense. His cool, confident assurance that you can handle the responsibility of owning a potentially lethal weapon if you avail yourself of a little training and purchase the "correct" gun, may be exactly what you want to hear. After all, you have good judgment. You are a very careful person who does not plan to hurt anybody. You just want to be safe.

The salesman is apt to be armed with a few stories, some of them quite true, of good guys shooting the bad guys, saving lots of lives and saving the state lots of prosecution and incarceration money. Indeed, the purchase of his product may actually save your kids from the deranged nut who is running out of control. It could conceivably result in your avoidance of the need to live out the rest of your life as a quadraplegic, devastated by bullet-inflicted spinal injuries. It could give you a way to fight back if someone attacks you. If only there were some way to know if it would work out as planned, that is, if the need ever arises...

The dealer is not likely to tell you about the man who purchased a gun for his protection and then accidently shot his own son or daughter. It's not that the salesman is a bad fellow. He very likely believes in the safety of his product and the wisdom of being prepared for any eventuality, especially the high probability these days of being victimized by a criminal. You can never be too safe. He knows that some innocent people die because bullets hit the wrong people, but he also knows that it doesn't happen as often as some people claim. Guns, after all, save lives. If he didn't believe that, then he wouldn't be selling them.

Another available source for the answer as to whether or not you should buy a gun for your personal protection or the protection of your family is the local grocery store, drug store, discount store or convenience store or any other place where you can buy a gun magazine. These enticing publications often feature ego-enhancing stories about the bold, well armed, law-abiding citizens who thwart criminals while they protect the innocent.

An endless array of new products promoted for their accuracy, efficiency and dependability engulfs the reader in the assumption that his purchases are a significant contribution to the reduction and even the prevention of crime. The accuracy, efficiency and dependability, of course, are in the killing only of bad guys. This is, perhaps, quite unfair. Most guns are purchased for sporting purposes, say, to hunt deer, elk, rabbits, javelena, squirrels, pheasant, doves or quail. Is there anything wrong with that? What is wrong with shooting as a sport, often a family sport? The answer is that there is nothing wrong with sports shooting if it is done safely and in accordance with the laws that apply.

Sports weapons and their use are not the issues here. The issue to be considered here involves, primarily though not exclusively, the millions of handguns being sold to people who are propagandized into believing that they are safer if they are armed. Certainly, it's unrealistic to expect the gun retailer who is, after all, a businessman, to emphasize the dangers over and above the benefits of the products he sells.

One might hope for this, just as one might hope that the cigarette distributor would stress the dangers of his products to the point that few would buy them, or the alcohol salesman would discuss the national problem of alcoholism so adversely that no one would buy his bourbon. One might hope for a realistic picture presented to the customer, but it just doesn't happen.

The problem persists. Should you buy a gun? Will you be glad that you did or will you be wishing that you hadn't? All that you need in order to come up with a suitable answer to this dilemma is the superhuman ability to do something that no one can do, namely, accurately predict the future.

If you do buy a gun and successfully use it to dissuade a criminal, then you will be glad you had the wisdom to arm yourself. If, on the other hand, you buy a gun, then one day as you shove it into your pocket it goes off and leaves you reproductively disadvantaged, you may feel that the salesman's suggestions were ill-advised. Gun ownership was not such a neat idea.

All you need to know in order to decide whether or not to buy that gun is precisely what will happen if you do and what will happen if you don't. The problem is that you can't predict the future as well as the gun dealer and the magazine publishers seem to do. You just don't have any way to know. It's a gamble, at best. Worth the risk? Yes, if it turns out the way you had it planned. No, if it turns out wrong. However, you don't know which it will be.

It's like trying to decide whether or not to use your last ten dollars to buy a roll of quarters to play the casino's slot machines. If one of those quarters pays off in lots of dollars, then it was really worth the gamble. If you lose the entire roll, the decision was a bad one. All you really needed was the ability to predict the future. If you had that, you'd surely end up rich. Here's to the best of luck...

Of course, most people who buy guns do not end up confronting a criminal or shooting a loved-one or friend. For the majority of owners their experience with a gun is a pleasant one, not resulting in threat or harm. The odds, fortunately, are very much in favor of becoming a safe and satisfied customer.

No mature, well-intentioned law-abiding citizen would buy a gun thinking that the purchase would result in sadness. If he thought that the gun would kill a relative or a friend by accident, he wouldn't buy it. If he knew that his gun purchase would endanger his kids, he would think twice. He is convinced, instead, that gun ownership will result in positive consequences. The bad things that happen are likely to happen to someone else. Is he right? Yes, most of the time he *is* right.

Most of the time it's someone from another town who dies. Or from another neighborhood. Certainly, from another family. Most of the time it's another routine story on the evening news or in the local newspaper. Tragic as they are in their effects on distant families, gun deaths in America are quite routine. At nearly 30,000 per year they are not rare, just routine.

The most challenging question as to whether or not you should invest in any gun solely for the protection of yourself and your family remains unanswered. Apparently, the answer depends on whom you ask. If you want a gun you will be inclined to talk to the people who sell guns. Then, you will get the answer you want. If you really want security for your family, you will be interested in the opinions of those who study family safety, those who provide statistics on accidents resulting in injury and in death by gunfire. You may not want those answers.

These can be seen as alarming figures that suggest that the odds of having your gun stolen and then used against you or some other victim far outweigh the odds of your ever using it to protect yourself or your family. The *New England Journal of Medicine* claimed in 1994 that the odds were forty-three to one that a gun kept in the home would kill a family member, a friend or an acquaintance rather than a criminal.

Of course, there are thousands of cases each year wherein the presence of a handgun prevented *anyone* from being shot. Then, there are the drive-by shootings, the drug-related killings, the planned homicides, the domestic arguments that end in fatalities, etc., where the presence of a handgun resulted in someone being shot.

If more law-abiding citizens were armed, could more lives be saved? If fewer people had guns, would we all be safer? Does buying a gun increase or decrease the security of your family? Who knows? Hope springs eternal! On any given day, many crimes may be prevented by armed citizens. On that same typical day approximately eighty people in America will die from gunfire. It would be a wonderful thing if you were the person who was armed and law-abiding in the time of need, the one soul who stood up to the criminal and was able to protect the innocent from violent aggression. How tragic would it be, however, to have to face the parents of any child killed by *your* gun, because on one occasion you forgot to lock it up? How would it feel if *your* untrained judgment contributed to the killing of an innocent person? Those unfortunate things would not happen to *you,* of course...

Should you buy a gun? Well, that's up to you. It could save your life. It could take your life. It could save your child, but it could cost you your child. Think about it. Not just before you shoot, but before you buy the gun.

Just as the spinning wheels could make you rich, they could also take your last ten dollars. But, with guns, the stakes are higher - a lot higher.

Chapter Twelve

Controversy

On the gun issue, there is controversy everywhere. Very few people stand in the middle of the issues related to gun control. Those who have lost loved-ones to gunfire are enraged by the resistance of members of the gun lobby to support what they see as reasonable regulations that could serve to reduce the carnage. They are apt to point to the words "well-regulated" in the Second Amendment and ask if arms are well-regulated today, as the Constitution mandates. Some even point to the tragic number of deaths of American soldiers that occurred during the recent war in Iraq and ask that the more than 4,230 lives be compared to the loss of over 28,600 by gunfire within the confines of the United States *in a single year.*

Conversely, others are equally enraged by any suggestion that gun control in any form would do anything other than restrict the rights of law-abiding citizens. Therefore, they are inclined to fight legislation that places limitations on the activities of gun manufacturers, dealers and private individuals. They point to the need for better enforcement of the existing laws rather than the enactment of new ones.

Lost in all of the conflict is the nature of the truth as it applies to such things as what the founding fathers intended as citizens' rights to bear arms, how the Supreme Court is interpreting the Second Amendment, whether or not more restrictive laws would actually have any tendency to reduce gun deaths, etc. At best, truth is a most elusive abstraction, more obvious to those who carry bias inversely proportionate to their level of sophistication. The truth is self-evident to those who have not taken it upon themselves to seriously consider the many variations of it. Yet, what is truth to one person is nothing more than illogical argumentation to another.

Those who seek a moderate view, one that considers both the need for more effective law enforcement *and* the need for more protective laws are criticized by those at each extreme for wanting to control too much or too little. One thing is very clear, however. The loss of human life to gunfire in America at the rate of 2,400 per *month* is a national disgrace. There is no justification for its simple acceptance as a price that must be routinely paid in order to assure the unregulated right of the citizenry to bear arms.

A weapons industry that is unregulated is no more beneficial to the security of the public than an unregulated automobile industry, an unregulated aircraft industry, an unregulated food and drug industry or an unregulated liquor or tobacco industry. Those who wish to legislate exclusive exemption from potential judicial litigation for those who manufacture and sell firearms should be encouraged to explain just what it is about their products that justifies that exclusion.

In the interest of public safety, the federal government mandates seat belts and air bags for all new automobiles, cockpit security doors for airliners, doctor regulated prescriptions for medications, inspections for meats and the regulation of the quality of other food products. Those regulations are in effect without any real prohibition of the consumers' right to seek judicial redress in the event of irresponsible product design, production or sales. Consumers who can be harmed by products can seek compensation through the courts. Yet, the gun folks seek to avoid the inconvenience of being held responsible within the court system for any potential defects or for any negligence on their part.

A major objective of the gun lobby involves proposed federal legislation against suits filed on behalf of gun victims. It is very interesting to note that House members voting to ban lawsuits against the manufacturers and distributors of weapons during the 2002 election campaign averaged more than $173 from the supporters of gun owners rights for every $1 those groups gave to opponents of the bill. Overall, gun rights groups gave $1.2 million to House members during the campaign while the supporters of gun control gave $27, 250.

A small percentage of gun distributors routinely circumvents the provisions of the Brady Law by selling weapons to "straw" buyers. This practice results in thousands of guns getting into the hands of people who should not have them. A noteworthy example is the *Bushmaster XM15* rifle used in the Beltway killings of twelve people in Washington, D C., in the Fall of 2002 by John Allen Mohammed and Lee Boyd Malvo.

The rifle was acquired from Bull's Eye Shooters Supply in Tacoma, Washington, though the store had no record of the sale. Should Bull's Eye be held accountable for the reckless manner m which it made the rifle available for crimmal behavior? "No," says the NRA "The Immunity bill should pass."

The NRA-supported immunity law would protect distributors like the Bull's Eye from having to face possible victim compensation based on negligent, irresponsible conduct in the transfer of arms. Should an immunity law passed by Congress protect reckless gun distributors from lawsuits? Should gunshot victims be denied their day in court? Apparently so.

Immunity from litigation for the gun industry is an unusual ploy, not characteristic of any other industry. If the yearly death toll involving aircraft in America were over 28,000, prohibition of court action against the industry would not be considered. No such action would be taken on behalf of the automobile industry. It is fair to ask what the unique nature of the gun in America is that justifies its special and exclusive exemption from the same considerations as all other consumer products.

Gun lobbyists worked the halls of Congress in support of legislation, notably HR 1036/S, that would have removed the opportunity for gunshot victims to seek compensation through the legal system. Their motivation for passage of such legislation is easily understood. They seek a shield against possible business bankruptcy that could occur because of frivolous lawsuits filed against them.

What is the motivation for those in Congress who would back such legislation? Is it that they are convinced that the public should not have the right to seek redress from gun distributors in the event of gross negligence or is it simply a matter of fear of standing up to the power of the gun lobby? The answer, of course, depends on whom you ask.

The Federal Assault Weapons Ban enacted m 1994 expired in late 2004. It was simply not renewed. A major objective of the gun lobby was to repeal the ban in spite of its overwhelming public support. Proponents for renewal and possible strengthening included Senator Dianne Feinstein in the United States Senate and Representatives Carolyn McCarthy and John Conyers in the United States House of Representatives.

Contested just before the upcoming 2004 national elections, both pro-gun and pro-gun control protagonists were expected to put considerable pressure on senators and congressmen and congresswomen for their much needed votes. The representatives of the NRA fought mightily for the repeal of the ban, whereas, members of the Brady Center To Prevent Gun Violence worked to build support for re-authorizing it with stronger limitations on the production and sales of Uzis, AK-47s and so called "Street Sweepers" with their potentially lethal rapid-fire capacities.

Should the ban have been reauthorized in stronger form or should it have been repealed? It depends on whom you ask. Should it have been allowed to die a quiet death by preventing it from reaching a final vote on the Senate floor or should it have been seen and supported as a sensible and logical extension of appropriate law intended to control the proliferation of rapid-fire weaponry? Again, the answer you get to this question depends on whom you ask.

Should people be allowed to carry concealed handguns anywhere they choose, including schools, bars, malls, grocery stores, parks, banks and sporting events? The NRA would like permissive CCW laws in all 50 states and would support federal law to reflect the freedom to be armed anywhere in public. The members of the Brady Campaign are resistant to this idea and are working to derail the attempts of the pro-gun lobby as they try to get more and more states to support this concept. Would you feel more secure knowing that the fellow behind you in line anywhere could be carrying a gun? Would you feel grateful that he is armed to protect you in the event that a bad guy should try to take advantage of you? Or, would you feel a bit safer if it were clearly against the law for anyone other than a law enforcement officer to be carrying a concealed weapon?

Would a national ballistics "fingerprint" database be helpful to members of law enforcement agencies intent on tracing bullets found at crime scenes? "Not so,' says the NRA representative, as he stresses the point that the firing of a weapon changes the characteristic print made by the barrel with each subsequent firing. Yet, the ballistic markings of bullets were successfully traced to the same Bushmaster rifle used in the killings of eight of the twelve victims in the D C area "Beltway" case. A national ballistics fingerprinting system sounds too much like weapons registration to the members of the gun lobby They will fight it regardless of the value it can provide to law enforcement agency personnel as they work to control the criminal element.

Another controversy involves the movement by some gun manufacturers toward the production of larger caliber handguns, notably a .50 caliber revolver designed by Smith & Wesson that is said to have three times the fire-power of a .44 magnum. Should gun shows be allowed on government property? Should those who purchase weapons at gun shows be exempted from the background checks required for purchasers of weapons from licensed gun dealers? What about weapons purchased from want ads in the daily newspapers?

Is the NRA really an "extremist" organization, as is claimed by the representatives of the Brady Center, or is it just an organization dedicated to the protection of individual rights that they claim are guaranteed by the Second Amendment of the United States Constitution? Who has the truth with regards to the issue of gun rights and the role of the government in the maintenance of the security of the American people? The answers to all of those important questions depend, of course, on whom you ask.

Bulletin: July 29, 2005 — Members of the United States Senate approved the immunity law and sent it to the president for his signature. The *"Protection of Lawful Commerce in Arms Act* (PLCA) is a federal law that gives the gun industry a broad nationwide immunity from legal responsibility for its actions. No other industry shares this immunity from tort liability.

Chapter Thirteen

Truth

Two Italian intellectuals became embroiled in a controversy regarding the leaning of the famous tower in Pisa, Italy. Both were learned men, well versed in history and on the subject of Romanesque architecture. The 187 foot-high tower leans to the south some fourteen feet at the top from being perfectly vertical, making it look precariously perched. It appears to be only months shy of disintegration.

"It leans to the right," said one of the brilliant men. "No, it surely leans to the left," said the other. Each was fully confident in the correctness of his view. "Any damned fool can see that it leans rightward," argued the first. "Well, I've got proof that it leans to the left," answered the second.

Soon each of the scholars was displaying the results of his exhaustive studies on the isue, quoting the intellectual writers who had written before his time and providing reports on soil analysis and gravitational forces that resulted in the leaning of the tower in, of course, the appropriate direction. "I have pictures that prove it leans to the right," said the first brilliant intellectual. "How can you deny this conclusive evidence? It's right before your eyes." "Well," said the other, "I have pictures that clearly show that the tower leans to the left, pictures taken through the finest optical lenses ever devised by man. And cameras don't lie."

Followers of these two great historians and intellectual researchers joined in the debate. Soon the University halls and lecture rooms were filled with the sounds of angry men who were scolding one another for their unwillingness to accept undeniable evidence in support of one view or another.

Each side had its version of the truth. Each side could back up the correct conclusions on the basis of research data. Members on each side knew that those on the other side were lacking in intellectual skill, letting their own biases prevent them from accepting factual evidence.

One century evolved into another. Frustrated by their inability to solve the matter of the leaning of the Tower of Pisa, the brilliant scholars finally decided to accept the fact that the issue would forever remain unsettled, not because scientific evidence was unavailable, but because scientific evidence *was* available. However, it was in conflict. It could lead to only one verifiable conclusion. The tower leans in both directions at once!

Of course, that's not possible. The "truth" of the matter is not dependent on the direction of the lean, but is instead, on the location of the one who studies it. If you stand to the west of the tower, it leans to the right. If you view it from the east, it leans to the left. So it is, with any issue that can be viewed from a variety of different angles. The direction of its lean depends on where you stand. You can even stand in some positions that result in no appearance of lean at all. "The United States Supreme Court leans too far to the left," say the conservatives, while the liberals are appalled at the way the conservatives are trying to increase its lean to the right.

Enamoured by the correctness of their own very carefully selected statistics on controversial issues, proponents begin to write and speak as though they have exclusive access to the truth. Theirs is the responsibility to reveal the truth, the truth that is hidden from the public by those with an opposing view. Some are so self-assured that they claim truth in the titles and subtitles of their writings, e. g.,*"If you want the truth that the anti-gunners don't want you to know..."* or *"Telling the Truth About Guns in America."*

The reality is that no one has the truth about guns or about gun control in America. No one knows for sure if gun control works or if it doesn't work. Everyone has an opinion. Everyone has supportive facts to back up that opinion, but no one has exclusive access to the truth. The problem is that the facts conflict with one another. The tendency is for anyone with a point of view to weed out those facts that are not supportive while proclaiming loudly about those that are.

Reading amidst the profusion of conflicting ideas about gun control, one can hardly escape the feeling that a fact is nothing more than an intellectual opinion, often verified by statistically significant data that are carefully selected in accordance with one's own personal bias. The establishment of statistical significance, even at the $P = \, < .01$ level of confidence is not the same as the establishment of truth, notably when the data are selective.

A disturbing implication endorsed by some who would lean too heavily on statistical data for support of their arguments is the idea that laws must be shown to be significantly effective in controlling criminal behavior before serious consideration is given to their enactment. Therefore, it is implied, specific gun laws should not be put into effect unless they are first proven effective in accordance with established statistical requirements.

If that step is prerequisite, then no drunk driving laws, for instance, should be enacted unless and until it can be shown statistically that they reduce drunk driving. No drug laws should be enacted without proving that the drug problem is less in areas with the laws than it is in areas where the laws are not in effect.

Should federal laws that require the use of seat belts in automobiles be considered in spite of the absence of hard statistical evidence (significant at the P <.01 level of confidence) that clearly supports their effectiveness? Indeed, if significant statistical t-tests must be prerequisite to the enactment of laws used to control all sorts of criminal behavior, then very few laws are likely to be enacted, let alone enforced.

Those who use their book titles, subtitles, text or carefully selected statistical compilations to claim that they have the truth are not any more likely to have the truth than is anyone else. They should feel encouraged to express their opinions and to report on their research evidence, but they are wise if they moderate their righteous claims of truthfulness. On the issue of gun control, their conclusions are more apt to depend on where they are standing than on any exclusive access they have to the truth.

Chapter Fourteen

What's next?

Is it possible to predict the trends for the next few years as the gun controversies rage on? The gun lobbyists push for more states to pass concealed-carry laws. Gun advocates even support national legislation that would permit concealed-carry in all 50 states. Will legislators in sufficient numbers support this trend? Would the president sign such a law? Would the courts uphold it? Should it be illegal for business employers to prevent employees from carrying weapons to work? The NRA apparently thinks so. They will soon be promoting a "take your gun to work" law as an extension of the carry-concealed movement.

What about the assault-weapons ban? Will a new administration seek to renew it? The conservative Bush administration let the renewal effort languish and die, responding to the pressure from the National Rifle Association. Does this mean there will be no future attempts to reinstate it - even in more comprehensive ways?

Then, there's the immunity law. That's the law that limits the right of those offended by gun violence from pursuing redress through the court systems by filing suits (called frivolous by gun lobbyists) against gun manufacturers and distributors. Surely, immunity legislation will be challenged by organizations such as the Brady Center To Prevent Gun Violence. Will judges uphold legislated limitations on the right of injured persons to be heard in courts of law? Who can predict the future? There's no way to know if the conservative trend toward the NRA-supported objectives will continue or if that trend will be turned around after a new administration takes hold in the year 2009. All that can be assured is that the power struggle will continue, with gun rights advocates seeking more and more gun freedoms and less conservative politicians advocating more control over factors that they feel are contributing to the problem of increasing national violence.

Some would argue that traditionally conservative administrations are often followed by those that are more centrist in nature. This change in emphasis is often referred to as a trend toward "moderation," although who is moderate and who is not depends greatly on whom you ask. There is much more to the issue of immunity for gun makers and distributors than just the process of protecting them from frivolous lawsuits. The implications of immunity legislation are quite profound. To put it mildly, there is more here than meets the ear.

Consider this: Conservatives have often decried the tendency for judges to usurp the responsibilities of the the legislators at both the federal and state levels by "legislating from the bench." The conservative views the separation of powers established in the constitution as highly significant in the maintenance of appropriate balance of influence between the three major divisions of government. The executive, legislative and judicial branches of government were intended to operate independently, each one providing a check against potential excesses on the part of the others. When judges encroach on the responsibilities of legislators by making law, rather than interpreting it, conservatives get very upset. This is especially true when the making of the law favors liberal causes. A clear example of this was seen in the conservative reaction to the 1973 Supreme Court opinion on abortion in Roe v. Wade. The endorsment by the Court of the right to choose an abortion (up until the seventh month of pregnancy) was seen by conservatives as usurpation of the right of legislators to establish laws that would protect the life of the unborn. Judges, the conservatives continue to argue, should interpret the law, not make new law.

What does all of this have to do with the immunity law that now prevents injured or offended citizens from seeking redress against gun makers and distributors? Many will claim that the immunity law also violates the concept of the separation of powers between the branches of government. It does so, they will claim, by restricting citizen access to the courts when it is established tradition for the courts, not legislators to decide which cases are to be heard. The immunity law is apt to be seen not as a case of "legislation from the bench," but instead as a reverse case of "judgment from the legislators' desks." The usurpation of the court's prerogative to select which cases are to be heard is apt to rankle the sensitivities of many judges who, given the opportunity, will seek to overturn the law on constitutional grounds. Conservatives who demand respect for the citizens' constitutional right to keep and bear arms seem minimally concerned for the constitutional right of citizens to be heard before the courts.

It's quite likely that the immunity law will be overturned, first in a lower court, then in appeal at the district court level. Then it is likely that the reversal of the immunity law will be upheld by the Supreme Court under the principle of stare decisis (Latin meaning: "Let the decision stand"). The Supreme Court may not even agree to hear the case.

This eventuality, should it prevail, would add significantly to the burdens of the gun lobbyists who must support the legislative removal of judicial oversight regarding who may file law suits - clearly a court function, not a legislative one. Are the justices apt to let senators, congressmen and congresswomen decide who may argue cases before them? Not likely.

Added to this is the challenge the gun lobbyists have of defending the stated individual rights view of the Second Amendment in the absence of federal judicial support, especially since the release of the opinions of the Ninth Circuit Court judges in Silveira v. Lockyer (Dec., 2002).

Perhaps the gun lobbyists have been misrepresenting the Second Amendment for decades with their claim of a guaranteed constitutional right for individuals to keep and bear aims. Or, is it the other way around? Have the gun control advocates been misleading the public with their claim that the right to bear arms is only constitutionally guaranteed for those who are in some way linked to service in a well- regulated militia? If the United States Supreme court were to hear arguments on both sides of the issue, what decision would prevail? *

* In June of 2008, the Supreme Court did make that decision. By a 5—4 vote, the court decided the Second Amendment issue on the side of an *individual* right. An in-depth analysis of this most significant decision is presented in the next chapter of this book.

Chapter Fifteen

So Sayeth the Court - A Momentous Decision

It seems highly unlikely that the United States Supreme Court could have avoided consideration of the many controversial issues surrounding possible interpretations of the Second Amendment for a period as long as seventy years. Yet, from 1939 (see *United States v. Miller,* 307 U.S. 174, 1939) to 2008, the issues were considered only at the inferior federal court levels in spite of the intense argumentation that prevailed in the public arena. During those years, lower court decisions seemed to favor a collective interpretation of the amendment as opposed to one that supported the right to bear arms as an individual right guaranteed for the average American citizen. Indeed, at the lower court levels, the individual rights view has been rejected by the Fourth, Sixth, Seventh, Ninth and Tenth Circuits. The First, Second, Third and Eighth Circuits also have issued difinitive rulings rejecting the individual rights view.

The amendment itself can be seen as supporting either interpretation, depending on one's personal preference. Even a rather cursory perusal of the wording of the amendment reveals the fact that it is possible to find support for either the collective right interpretation (militia only) or for the right of the *individual* to keep and bear arms.

Ratified in 1791, the amendment reads as follows:

"A well-regulated Militia, being necessary to the security of free State, the right of the people to keep and bear arms shall not be infringed."

Seeing the issue as a collective right requires emphasis on the first phrase "A well-regulated Militia, being necessary to the security of a free State" as a preamble (called the prefatory clause) that states the purpose and reason for the remaining portion of the amendment, referred to as the operative clause. Proponents of the collective model argue that the right to bear arms is linked necessarily to militia involvement of the citizen. It is, therefore, not established as an individual right that is independent of that linkage.

Those who see the amendment as applicable to individual citizens, even those without any affiliation with some form of militia activity tend to ignore the first part and stress only the part that says "the right of the people to keep and bear arms shall not be infringed." The reference to the *people* is judged to include any law-abiding citizen, not just those who are connected to the militia in some way.

In 2008, the Supreme Court finally decided to hear a case that would settle the issue. Its opinion in the *District of Columbia v. Heller* case was released on June 28, 2008. The case stems from the fact that the District of Columbia has a law in effect that prohibits the possession of handguns. Under the D.C. law, it is a crime to carry an unregistered firearm although a one year license can be issued by the chief of police. Long guns must be kept unloaded and disassembled or bound by a trigger lock in the home.

Needless to say, this law was seen by some as a violation of the original intent of the founding fathers to protect the right of citizens as individuals to keep and bear arms. In a case heard and decided by the Court of Appeals for the D.C. Circuit *(Parker v. District of Columbia,* 478F. 3d 370) in March of 2007 a three judge panel by a vote of 2 — I held that the D.C. law was unconstitutional.

The law was said to be too restrictive and in clear violation of the Second Amendment. A significant part of the decision reads "The activities the amendment protects are not limited to militia service, nor is an individual's enjoyment of the right contingent upon his or her continued or intermittent enrollment in the militia." The requirement that all firearms be kept unloaded, disassembled or bound by a trigger lock was also rejected. A subsequent petition for an *en banc* (full court) rehearing was submitted in April of 2007 in an attempt to overturn the Parker decision, but it was denied by a 6 — 4 vote.

The United States Supreme Court was petitioned to hear the case and did agree on Nov. 20, 2007 to do so. At issue was whether or not the restrictive D.C. law violated Second Amendment rights of individuals, notably, those who are not affiliated with any state-regulated militia who want to keep firearms for private use in their homes. In effect, it questions if the Second Amendment does or does not guarantee an individual the right to keep and bear arms, absent any connection with an organized militia. For technical reasons, the case was renamed *District of Columbia et. al., v. Heller* (No.07-290). In the district, Dick Heller, a D.C. police officer, was denied a registration permit for a handgun that he wished to keep at home. The Supreme Court was to decide on constitutional grounds if that denial violated Heller's Second Amendment rights.

It's useful to study the make-up of the United States Supreme Court at the time of its judgment on the issue of collective versus individual Second Amendment rights. The Court is reasonably balanced between the conservative members in support of an individual right to keep and bear arms and those more liberal justices who see the amendment as requiring militia affiliation to guarantee that right.

Four justices lean toward the individual right view, namely, Antonin Scalia, Samuel Alito Jr., Clarence Thomas and the Chief Justice, John Roberts. Four others, namely, John Paul Stevens, Ruth Bader Ginsburg, David Souter and Stephen Breyer are more liberal and lean toward the collective right view. A ninth Supreme Court justice, Anthony Kennedy is often considered a "swing" voter who could have gone either way on his interpretation of Second Amendment rights.

The decision of the Court was released on June 26, 2008. Justice Kennedy sided with the conservative members of the court to provide a 5 —4 ruling in favor of the individual right view. Justice Antonin Scalia wrote the majority opinion. Quoting Justice Scalia, "The Second Amendment protects an individual right to possess a firearm unconnected with service in a militia, and to use that firearm for traditionally lawful purposes, such as defense within the home." In keeping with that right, the Court decided that the D.C. handgun ban and a related trigger lock requirement as well as required weapons disassembly amount to prohibitions on an entire class of arms that Americans overwhelmingly choose for the lawful purpose of self defense. As such, the requirements are held as unconstitutional.

After nearly seventy years, the United States Supreme Court has finally provided an opinion that solves the issue of collective versus individual right for every citizen to keep and bear arms. The reaction to the Court decision reveals a great expression of relief and enthusiasm by representatives of the gun lobby intent on using it as a springboard for the repeal of as many existing gun laws as possible. Legal challenges to existing gun laws can be expected to appear in courts across the land as though the majority opinion serves to break down the constitutionality of many laws that restrict or otherwise regulate gun possession and use.

Mindful of this potential challenge of existing federal, state and local laws regulating weapons ownership and use, however, the Court qualified its position by adding the following provision: "Like most rights, the

Second Amendment right is not unlimited. It is not a right to keep and carry any weapon whatsoever in any manner whatsoever and for whatsoever purpose. For example, concealed weapons prohibitions have been upheld under the amendment or state analogues. The Court's opinion should not be taken to cast doubt on longstanding prohibitions on the possession of firearms by felons and the mentally ill, or laws forbidding the carrying of firearms in sensitive places such as schools and government buildings, or laws imposing conditions and qualifications on the commercial sale of arms. *Miller's* holding (1939) that the sorts of weapons protected are those in common use at the time finds support in the historical tradition of prohibiting the carrying of dangerous and unusual weapons."

It is important to note in this context that the Court appears not to challenge the licensing requirement for weapons enacted by the District of Columbia. "Because Heller conceded at oral argument that the D.C. licensing law is permissable if it is not enforced arbitrarily and capriciously, the Court assumes that a license will satisfy his prayer for relief and does not address the licensing requirement. Assuming he is not disqualified from exercising Second Amendment rights, the District must permit Heller to register his handgun and must issue him a license to carry it in the home."

The foregoing suggests considerable acceptance of most existing gun laws by the Court, even the requirement that a weapon be registered if that requirement is put into law by federal or any state or local government. While the United States Supreme Court with its *District of Columbia et al., v. Heller* decision has decided to support the operative clause of the Second Amendment by choosing individual right over collective right, the prefatory clause is still in efffect with its assertion that the right should be well-regulated. The Court did not recommend any significant reduction in other lawfully arranged regulations or limitations applied to gun ownership or use.

Established laws that regulate the availability of assault weapons, the carrying of concealed weapons, provide for gun-free "zones," or regulate the commercial sale of arms do not violate the Second Amendment to the United States Constitution. Conservative United States Supreme Court Justice Antonin Scalia, with a majority-supported opinion in *Heller* announced that a broad range of America's gun laws including required registration (where enacted) remain "presumptively legal."

So sayeth the United States Supreme Court.

About the Author

The author is Emeritus professor of psychology and behavioral statistics with academic training that includes A.A., B.S., M.A. and Ph.D degrees in experimental psychology with graduate level minors in criminology and business. He is well-qualified to present a scholarly representation of the many controversial sides of America's gun issues from both a behavioral and legal point of view.

Dr. Lucier is especially interested in a significant development in the United States Supreme Court pertaining to the question of Second Amendment gun rights. The recent pronouncement expressed in the case *of District of Columbia et. al.,v. Heller* (2008) has overturned a historically recorded trend lasting for over seventy years. That trend, shown quite consistently at inferior court levels upheld the strong argument that the constitutionally guaranteed right to keep and bear arms was necessarily linked to membership in a well-regulated militia.

The reversal of that militia linkage requirement by the Supreme Court offers an opportunity for potential challenge of many gun laws presently in effect. Dr. Lucier is especially interested in the likelihood of significant legislative and judicial changes that might occur with the advent of the new adminstration that took office in 2009.

Index

About the Book

For generations it has been assumed by most people that the Second Amendment to the United States Constitution guarantees the right of individual citizens to keep and beararms. Approximately 70% of all Americans and virtually all gun enthusiasts support this basic assumption.

The National Rifle Association resists much gun legislation using the argument that restrictive laws often infringe on the right to gun ownership established by the founding fathers as a significant part of the Bill of Rights. Others claim, however, that the Second Amendment pertains only to the right of the individual *states* to form well-regulated militias.

The "individual" vs. "collective" rights controversy has been heatedly argued in the courts since 1939, resulting in a strong leaning toward denial of the individual rights view, notably in the federal appeals courts.

However, an opinion released by the United States Supreme Court in *District of Columbia et. al., v. Heller* in 2008 (No. 07-290) challenged the lower court opinions by deciding the issue in favor of the individual right interpretation of the Second Amendment. Several lower court opinions and also an analysis of the deciding Supreme Court case are reported in this informative book. An in-depth review of these cases should be prerequisite to any claim of sophistication regarding the issue of gun rights in America.

Free Preview

The Second Amendment to the United States Constitution, ratified in 1791, reads as follows:

> "A well-regulated Militia, being necessary to the security
> of a free State, the right of the people to keep an bear Arms
> shall not be infringed."

What does the amendment mean? How should it be interpreted? Were the people mentioned in the amendment intended to be all of the people, or just those who were members of a well-organized militia? Are individual citizens guaranteed a constitutional right to keep and bear arms? Or, was the intended purpose of the amendment limited only to the establishment of State militias?

The controversy rages on. Three possible schools of thought form the basis for debate on the issue. First, let's consider the more traditional "individual rights model" that holds that the Second Amendment guarantees to individual private citizens a fundamental right to possess and use firearms for any purpose at all, subject only to limited government regulation. It is the view that is supported by the National Rifle Association and most firearms enthusiasts.

The second variant is often referred to as the "limited individual rights" model. Individuals under this model maintain a constitutional right to possess firearms insofar as such possession bears a reasonable relationship to militia service. This model confirms militia association as prerequsite to that right.

The third possible interpretation is usually called the "collective model." It asserts that the Second Amendment right to bear arms guarantees only the right of the people to maintain well-regulated militias. It does not protect the right of any citizen to own or possess weapons if that person is unaffiliated with a well-organized militia. This is, of course, the position most resisted by the NRA.

Over the past seventy years, only one significant pronouncement had been made on the issue of a Second Amendment right to keep and bear arms by the United States Supreme Court, namely in the case of *United States v. Miller*, 307 U.S. 174 (1939), a case related to the transportation of sawed-off shotguns in interstate commerce. The court rejected a challenge to the right to transport those weapons. In the the *Miller* opinion, the court concluded:

> "In the absence of any evidence tending to show that possession or use of a shotgun having a barrel of less than eighteen inches in length at this time has some reasonable relationship to the preservation or efficiency of a well-regulated militia, we cannot say that the Second Amendment guarantees the right to keep and bear such an instrument. Certainly, it is not within judicial notice that this weapon is any part of the ordinary military equipment or that its use could contribute to the common defense."

Subsequent to this pronouncement and through the next seven decades, the tendency in the lower level (inferior) federal courts has been to support the limited individual rights and collective model interpretations of the Second amendment, as in the case of *Lewis v. the United States*, 445 U.S. 55,65 n. 8 (1980). *Lewis* characterized the *Miller* holding as follows:

> "The Second Amendment guarantees no right to keep and bear a firearm that does not have some reasonable

relationship to the preservation or efficiency of a well-regulated militia."

In a rare, but noteworthy exception to the lower courts' support of collective rights, the Fifth Circuit Court in the case of *United States v. Emerson*, (No. 01-8780, at 19 n.3., 2001) held that the Second Amendment "does protect the rights of individuals, including those persons who are not members of any militia or engaged in active military service or training, to possess and bear their own firearms, subject to reasonable restrictions."

Gleefully supporting the *Emerson* opinion in support of an individual right, NRA representatives were set back the following year by the countering opinion in the Ninth Circuit Court of Appeals in *Silveira v. Lockyer* (No. 01-15098, D.C. No. CV-00-00411-WBS, 2002) that concluded as follows:

> "The historical context of the Second Amendment and the debates relevant to its adoption demonstrate that the founders sought to protect the survival of Free States by ensuring the existence of effective State militias, not by establishing an individual right to possess firearms. An examination of the historical context surrounding the enactment of the Second Amendment leaves us with little doubt that the proper reading of the amendment is that embodied in the collective rights model."

The foregoing suggests an intense sustained controversy that has lasted for over seventy years, leaving the issue of Second Amendment rights unclarified and unresolved. Will the issue ever be settled? The answer is "Yes, it will. Yes, it has been." In its first major pronouncement on the issue of Second Amendment rights since 1939, The United States Supreme Court has at last addressed the issue and drawn definitive conclusions. In June of 2008, the Court issued its opinion in the case of the *District of Columbia, v. Heller*, (478 F. 3d 370).

Dick Heller, a D.C. police officer, had been denied a registration permit for a handgun that he wished to keep at his home. The Supreme Court was to decide on constitutional grounds if that denial violated Heller's Second Amendment right to keep and bear arms. At issue was whether or not a city, county, state or district could enact a law that prohibited any law-abiding citizen the right to own a gun. It was an issue that led directly to the need for appropriate interpretation of the Second Amendment, a near perfect case to test its scope and purpose, a forum for in-depth, scholarly investigation of the intent of the founding fathers as well as the implications for public policy with regard to weapons management in America.

In this book, the Court's opinion in the *Heller* case is reviewed and analyzed in search of those many elusive answers necessary for an understanding of Second Amendment rights. The Court has decreed its interpretation of Second Amendment objectives with its momentous opinion in the *District of Columbia v. Heller* case. That opinion was released on June 26, 2008.

So sayeth the Court.